MW00354983

Stop Panic Attacks

23 Powerful Relaxation Techniques to End Panic
Attacks, Keep Calm and Overcome Phobias. Regain
Control of Your Life and Your Peace of Mind

Derick Howell

© **Copyright Derick Howell 2020 - All rights reserved.**

The content contained within this book may not be reproduced, duplicated or transmitted without direct written permission from the author or the publisher.

Under no circumstances will any blame or legal responsibility be held against the publisher, or author, for any damages, reparation, or monetary loss due to the information contained within this book. Either directly or indirectly. You are responsible for your own choices, actions, and results.

Legal Notice:

This book is copyright protected. This book is only for personal use. You cannot amend, distribute, sell, use, quote or paraphrase any part, or the content within this book, without the consent of the author or publisher.

Disclaimer Notice:

Please note the information contained within this document is for educational and entertainment purposes only. All effort has been executed to present accurate, up to date, and reliable, complete information. No warranties of any kind are declared or implied. Readers acknowledge that the author is not engaging in the rendering of legal, financial, medical or professional advice. The content within this book has been derived from various sources. Please consult a licensed professional before attempting any techniques outlined in this book.

By reading this document, the reader agrees that under no circumstances is the author responsible for any losses, direct or indirect, which are incurred as a result of the use of the information contained within this document, including, but not limited to, — errors, omissions, or inaccuracies.

Your Free Gift

This book includes a free bonus booklet. All information on how you can quickly secure your free gift can be found at the end of this book. It may only be available for a limited time.

TABLE OF CONTENTS

INTRODUCTION

Panic attacks are scary, though you don't necessarily have to be in a scary situation to have a panic attack. For example, you could be on a hike, at a restaurant, or asleep in bed, then all of a sudden you feel a strong surge of fear ripple through you. That fear triggers physical symptoms like a pounding heart, sweating shortness of breath, nausea, chest pain, and trembling. This terrifying feeling can last between 5 to 20 minutes, and the worst thing is that you probably didn't see this scary thing before it happened; you were just doing your own thing when you were quickly overcome with these feelings.

There is no known cause for panic attacks, and people of all ages get them. The worst part is that panic attacks come with some pretty intense physical and psychological symptoms. These symptoms are so severe that a person who has a panic attack often ends up in the emergency room, scared for their life. Panic attacks are routinely misdiagnosed by the people who have them, but it isn't because they told a lie or exaggerated; they had very severe chest pains, they couldn't catch their breath, or they started to breathe shallow, short breaths that would leave them gasping for air. It is not surprising that your family members called an ambulance to take you to the hospital the first time they witnessed you having an attack.

While the doctor runs every test and finds that everything is in order, he approaches you with the news that you had a panic attack, which leaves you surprised. You thought you were going to die, and that this was just an overblown anxiety attack. You might even receive a visit from the on-call psychiatrist so they can evaluate you. What you will learn from this psychiatrist is that anxiety attacks are treatable.

There are numerous treatments for panic attacks, including changing your mindset, preventive measures for stopping a panic attack during the event itself, counseling, and other treatments. Anxiety and panic attacks can be cured! In fact, there are six therapeutic methods for treating anxiety attacks. In this book, we will be going over various strategies that can help you to get your life back. I will teach you the five steps of AWARE (acknowledge and accept the panic attack, wait and watch (or work), actions (that make you more comfortable), repeat, and end) This might not make sense to you now, but I will explain this technique and other techniques like it simply and understandably, so you can finally take charge of your panic attacks as soon as possible.

I used to experience panic attacks all the time, especially before a speaking engagement in front of crowds. I've learned how to manage them through the years and experience, and I will be sharing firsthand some of the techniques I've been using to stop those panic attacks. I even wanted to give up my speaking engagements and my job because I was scared of the next panic attack that I was going to have. However, I became determined to learn more about my panic attacks and do my best to get them to stop. I've lived through the heart-stopping panic and the frightening feeling that I was going to die, and plan to teach you the techniques and strategies I have used to cope. I was able to do that, and now I would like to share with you what I learned.

In this book, you will learn how to stop and control your panic attacks, calm yourself down during the most intense attacks, and about some powerful relaxation techniques. I am confident that you can overcome your phobias and cure yourself of panic attacks!

This book is going to give you various strategies that you can use to stop your panic attacks, and I will also tell you about the different therapies that are most effective for dealing. I will even help you with finding a therapist and what questions you can ask them when you go to your first session.

You are not alone in having panic attacks—once you start sharing the fact that you have panic attacks with your friends and family, you might discover that one of them has also had panic attacks. You will find that many men and women from different walks of life have all had panic attack issues. One of the most important things to remember is that you need to reach out to someone in order to ask for help. Reading this book can be a start to reaching out; you may also want to share this book with your family, so they can understand how to help you, and you can even bring this book with you to therapy. While in therapy, you can discuss the techniques within and decide which ones work best for you.

This book isn't meant to be a substitute for medical treatment; it is very important that your doctor clears you of any other potential medical conditions that could be causing your symptoms and experiences. However, once you can confirm that you are having panic attacks, you can start using the strategies in this book to help you through these overwhelming panic attacks. I want you to have the best information possible, so I have included in this book the best therapies and medications that are effective for treating panic attacks.

When you do go to a therapist or a psychiatrist, it is good to know about the medications that they can provide. There are many different categories of medications that can be prescribed for anxiety, and this book will provide you a list of the various types of medications that can be prescribed for anxiety.

There is no set combination of medications that can be prescribed to you. In fact, finding the right medications for you can be a hit or miss ordeal. The psychiatrist will listen to you about the type of anxiety you're feeling; specifically, what your triggers are and how you react to your anxiety. Then the psychiatrist will try to match the best type of medication for your unique reaction to anxiety. The psychiatrist will schedule a follow-up in a month or less to know how you are faring. This is an important check-up because this appointment will be when you can discuss any side effects you are experiencing and how effective the medicine is to your anxiety. During this exam, your psychiatrist may increase your dosage or ask you to try other medications.

This book delivers by giving you a list of medications and describing each category for you, so when you go to a psychiatrist, you are well-informed and can participate in deciding what medication you are going to take.

By reading this book, you can cure your panic attacks and alleviate your symptoms. Panic attacks don't have to go on forever—you can do something to stop them, and this book will help you do just that.

You can find relief now—right this minute. If you are currently experiencing a panic attack, go to Chapters 4 and 5 to find out how you can stop an attack by remaining calm during that intense panic attack. Otherwise, feel free to peruse through this book to gain crucial knowledge for understanding and curing your panic attacks.

CHAPTER ONE:

How Does a Panic Attack Feel?

Panic attacks are not new to society—in the past, people who suffered from panic attacks were called nervous or high strung. At first, panic attacks were thought of as more of a character flaw than a mental illness. Very often, people who suffered from panic attacks were hospitalized or, in some tragic cases, institutionalized. Panic attacks have always been around, but only just recently are we beginning to understand their dynamics.

Panic attacks do not exist in a bubble; everyday women and men all experience panic attacks. For example, a person can get nervous about an upcoming exam or certification, or they could become nervous about a tax audit or an upcoming social event. Does this necessarily mean that you are suffering from panic attacks?

In this chapter, you will learn about three people who suffer from panic attacks. These three people could be anyone that you would cross paths with on the street, at any time. What they have in common is the fact that their panic attacks interfere with their daily living. These three examples are only a tiny slice or cross-section of panic attack examples. The purpose of these examples is to illustrate what a panic attack feels like.

Alice and Her Panic Attack

Alice sat in her car and tried to wait for her heart to stop pounding. She was outside the hospital where her newborn grandson was waiting to meet her. Alice was short of breath and shaking, and she felt that, if she got out of the car, she would surely die. The hospital was huge, and the maternity ward was at the furthermost end of the hospital. How would she be able to get there? She opened the door and stepped out of the car, holding on to the door. Her heart pounded harder and her knees were weak. She tried to take a step but felt dizzy. Immediately, she got back into her car. By now, she was sweating profusely and shivering in the freezing wind. When she reached for her phone to call her son, she dreaded telling him that she couldn't go see her new grandson because of her panic attack. She started to cry—it isn't fair. She put the phone down because she started feeling some massive chest pain, and she feared that she was having a heart attack. She didn't know what to do; she was so scared of dying in her car, but where would she go? To the emergency room?

Alice knew from experience that she wasn't having a heart attack; she was having a panic attack. What would Alice do to get herself to calm down? Alice closed her eyes and gave herself five minutes to calm down, so she could then drive home. She was really looking forward to meeting her new grandson. Though this wasn't the first time this had happened to her, this was the first time her panic attack intervened during an important event.

The twenty minutes passed quickly, and she felt a bit calmer, so she started the car to drive away. Alice tried not to look at the hospital as she drove and she still felt horrible, but the further she got from the hospital, the more she felt the tight band around her chest loosen. What was she going to tell her son about not being able to get out of her car and go see her grandson? Alice sniffled and wiped the tears away, feeling dejected, as this visit was very important to her. Why did she feel this way? She wished that there was something she could do to stop the panic attacks, but who could help her? It would change her life for the better if only she knew what to do.

Bradley and His Panic Attack

Bradley sat in the outer waiting room, waiting to be called for his job interview. He had been preparing for this interview for two weeks; he was well-qualified for the job, and he had even done some outstanding volunteer work in a similar field. Bradley was a great guy, but he had been doing far too many interviews in the past few months. Every interview ended similarly: with him not getting the job.

The cute receptionist told Bradley that it was his turn to be interviewed, and he found himself getting up too fast and feeling dizzy. He closed his eyes and took a deep breath, waiting for the dizziness to go away. The cute receptionist held the door open for him and, in the room, the human resources director and the lead engineer waited for Bradley to take a seat. Bradley felt like there was something stuck in his throat; he swallowed hard, but it didn't go away. He suddenly felt moisture under his armpits and back. Bradley gave a nod to the men before he sat down.

The room felt really hot, and he noticed that his hands were shaking. The men asked their first question, and though Bradley tried to answer, his brain felt empty. Instead, he said something that he had practiced for weeks—a computer-like recitation of his experience. As he talked, he felt a shortness in his breath. The men looked at Bradley strangely, which did nothing to alleviate the pain that was beginning to grow in his chest. It felt like an elephant was standing on his chest. He had to leave the interview as soon as possible, or something really bad would happen, he was sure.

The truth of the matter was that the worst was happening to Bradley right at that minute. Bradley stood and gathered his briefcase, causing the men to stare at him, shocked. The interview ended with Bradley walking out the door, feeling light-headed and faint, though he made it out of the building and into his car. This was interview number 20 that he had just botched up. He sat in his car and tried to calm down but couldn't, as his heart was beating way too fast and he was trembling. He couldn't catch his breath. At that moment, Bradley felt like he was dying. He put his head down on the wheel and prayed.

Lisa and Her Service Dog

Lisa was doing her laundry in the apartment laundry room. She had one load washing and another load in the dryer, and along with her in the laundry room was her service dog. She opened her book and started reading; then, from out of nowhere, she heard an extremely loud sound, startling her. What happened? Within minutes, she was perspiring, her heart beating out of her chest. She started feeling short of breath. Her dog Sandy got close to Lisa's purse, causing Lisa to remember that she had some medication in there. Within minutes of taking the medication, Lisa started feeling better. Sandy stayed close, and Lisa pet her to calm down. This was what it was like when you had learned what to do when a panic attack happens to you.

Amanda's Story

In her first semester of college, Amanda was the victim of abuse by her high school sweetheart. Jealous that Amanda was making new friends, Josh became increasingly hostile toward Amanda. She did her best to include Josh in her new life, but he was never satisfied. Then, one night, after going to a party on campus, Josh, who was fully inebriated, became violent while dropping Amanda off at her dorm. Fueled by jealousy, Josh began to punch and kick Amanda until she was unconscious. Bystanders who witnessed the violence called the police and an ambulance.

This was a night that Amanda would never forget.

Severe panic attacks often plague a person after they experience a violent or traumatic event. Amanda struggled when she returned to school, and loud noises triggered Amanda's panic attacks. Those panic attacks were a symptom of her Post Traumatic Stress Disorder (PTSD).

Various different situations can cause panic attacks, and there are many degrees to the severity of a panic attack; you don't have to have PTSD to suffer through them.

In order for us, as readers and listeners, to have a better understanding of what it is like to have a severe panic attack, Amanda agreed to answer some questions and have those answers included in this book.

What was it like for you after the attack?

A few days after I got home from the hospital, I didn't feel like myself. I found myself crying for what seemed like no reason, and I felt more depressed than I ever have felt. When it came time to go back to school, I just couldn't go. I stayed in my room and refused to come out. It seemed like I was afraid of everything, even my own shadow.

Did you eventually leave your room?

Yes, my parents convinced me that I had to go back to school because if I didn't go back to school, it would be like Josh took something valuable from me. I went back, but it wasn't easy.

Did you get anxious when you were on campus?

I did more than just get anxious. I had a full-blown panic attack when I crossed the quad to get to my class. Being around a large group of people talking loudly was a trigger for me. I completely lost it in the quad.

What happened?

I started to feel like my heart was going to pop out of my chest because it was beating so hard. I started shaking and I couldn't breathe right. Eventually, I hyperventilated and fainted. It was a humiliating experience.

After this experience, my mother found a therapist for me and I began to work on my panic attack issues. It was really hard for me because I isolated myself from everyone: my parents, my teachers, and even my friends.

How long did this go on?

A few months went by. I grew increasingly isolated and even started to drink and smoke pot on my own. Then, I got tired of always being alone. My friends were doing well in school and getting involved in all sorts of activities, and I was just staying at home feeling more depressed. I even thought about suicide.

Did you have panic attacks during this period?

Yes, I did, every time I had to leave the house. They weren't as severe as the collapse in the quad, but they were serious enough to get in the way of my daily life. My parents insisted I go to school, but just getting up in the morning and dressing for school was an ordeal. I would get paralyzed with panic attacks. When my parents drove me to school, I would feel my heart pounding outside my chest and I had this big fear that I was going to lose control and do something really crazy.

Are you still experiencing panic attacks?

No, I am much better now. Therapy really helped me to get control over the panic attacks.

How did therapy help?

Well, I learned all about the things that triggered my panic attacks, and then my therapist helped me to find ways to cope with my panic attacks. I guess I'll never forget what happened to me, but it isn't as vivid to me anymore. Also, the things that trigger me are getting less and less.

What types of tools did your therapist give you to be able to deal with your panic attacks?

I learned all about being mindful and not pushing myself when I am uncomfortable in a situation. My therapist recommended that I start a journal to explore my feelings, and this helped an awful lot. She also taught me some breathing exercises and ways to cope that I can do when I begin to feel a panic attack coming on.

Do you feel 100% now?

I don't know if I'll ever feel better, but I am a lot more confident now. When I do have bad days—and I do get bad days— I have learned to just take it easy and be kind to myself.

What would you tell others who are experiencing panic attacks?

I would say to do everything you can to learn techniques that will help you with your panic attacks.

Panic Attacks and Their Symptoms

All four of these people suffered from panic attacks but in different ways for various distinct reasons; yet, they all seemed to manifest panic attacks similarly. Just as the reasons for the panic attacks differed, the same goes for the symptoms that happened during an attack or episode. A person can have all the symptoms or only a few.

The duration and intensity of a panic attack can also vary, but the one true thing that people with panic disorder have is that they feel terrible and that they cannot carry on with their usual activities.

The physical symptoms that are most often felt include accelerated heart rate, trembling or shaking, shortness of breath, chest pain, feeling unsteady, and sweating. The psychological feelings can range from a fear of losing control and a fear of dying.

In the next chapter, I will go into more detail about the cause and symptoms of panic attacks. I will also provide you with information that can help you figure out if you are one who is suffering from panic attacks.

Chapter Summary

This chapter detailed four people who struggle with panic attacks, and each person dealt with panic attacks in their own way. In this chapter, we learned that:

- Panic attacks have devastating symptoms that can disrupt a person's daily life.
- Panic attacks can be triggered by trauma or stressful situations.
- Panic attacks can be treated with medication and therapy.

In the next chapter, we will be going over the causes and symptoms of panic attacks—why they happen, physical and psychological symptoms, and panic attack characteristics.

CHAPTER TWO:

Panic Attacks 101

Back when humans were trying to stave off wild animals and other natural threats, anxiety was an important emotion to have. Anxiety demanded that one keep alert and cautious about the world around them, and it was a response to stress or a situation that proved traumatic. Although we are not generally staving off dangerous wild animals on a daily basis, there are still a lot of things to be wary of, including that all-important job interview or meeting your partner's parents for the first time. We will occasionally respond to these situations with fear and almost always with nervousness.

The problem with anxiety is that it can become so extreme that you find yourself *chronically* anxious, or anxious all the time. In this case, you would have so much anxiety that it ends up interfering with your everyday life. If the anxiety becomes this sort of problem, you might have an anxiety disorder. The question is: will you have a panic attack if you have an anxiety disorder?

According to the Anxiety and Depression Association of America (ADAA), a panic attack is an onset of an intense fear that gets in the way of functioning normally. People without an anxiety disorder still feel anxious and nervous, but it does not interfere with their functioning, and they are generally able to endure stressful situations. A person who experiences panic attacks will often feel physically ill in the same situations. This person will have palpitations, a pounding heart, start shaking, have intense perspiration, and other uncomfortable physical and psychological feelings.

Panic attacks will keep people from doing things that have to be done; for example, such an individual may have difficulties going to work because they believe they might have a panic attack while riding an elevator, or they don't go to school because they have had a panic attack every time they took a test.

Is a Panic Attack the Same as an Anxiety Attack?

Although very similar, panic attacks are different from an anxiety attack, with the differences being intensity and timing. When you have an anxiety attack, the anxiety is still manageable and goes away after you get through the stressful situation. You may have the symptoms of a panic attack, like shortness of breath or an accelerated heart rate, but these symptoms go away after the stressful situation is resolved.

A panic attack has some of the same physical symptoms that an anxiety attack has, but these symptoms are more intense and they seem to happen unexpectedly or for reasons you can't explain. Panic attacks are unprovoked and unpredictable; they have more severe symptoms like shortness of breath, dizziness, and even nausea, and some people may even have very severe chest pains during a panic attack. The pain is so acute that these chest pains are often thought to be a heart attack.

Even though panic attacks can be unprovoked or unpredictable, a person can still have triggers that would cause an attack to occur. Bright lights and loud noises can make a person have a panic attack; for example, a person can walk into a situation where everything is calm, then some bright lights start flashing and loud music blares. Unexpectedly, this situation has now caused a panic attack, and they didn't expect to have this attack prior to it happening. Panic attacks also come with the fear of the next panic attack. As the fear is more acute, the person may try to avoid all bright lights in hopes that doing so will help them avoid the next panic attack; in essence, it is not the bright lights that a person fears in this situation, but the next panic attack. The next section will talk more in-depth about this phenomenon.

With an anxiety attack, you would generally know beforehand that the stressful situation is going to cause anxiety—a visit to your dentist can be so stressful that you surmise you will have an anxiety attack when you hear the drilling start and, in this case, it is the dentist that causes the anxiety, not the anxiety attack itself.

Anxiety Attacks vs. Panic Attacks

When you have an anxiety attack, it is still possible to get through the stressful situation. You may want to avoid the situation, but you would go ahead and work your way through it, as the anxiety is manageable. However, with panic attacks, you begin to have what is called **anticipatory anxiety**—worry or fear of having your next panic attack because they are overwhelming and unpredictable, and you believe it impossible to function or endure the next attack. When this happens, you begin to avoid any situation that might cause that panic attack.

Although panic attacks can be diagnosed, clinicians really don't know what causes them. You would think that, since you can recognize the symptoms, you would be able to tell the origins of an anxiety attack. An attack is much more than being stressed about something—you can easily understand why a situation

17

would provoke anxiety, but it may be harder to understand why a person would have a complete physical and psychological meltdown that would render them unfunctional. Researchers have not quite figured out just yet why a mental situation can turn into a severe physical reaction.

What Causes a Panic Attack

Even though clinicians don't know the cause, they still try to isolate what may have triggered the attack, and try to make educated guesses about the situation. For example, a person's genetics and major stress could be the cause of the attack. In some families, you could probably see a direct line of family members with a history of panic attacks so severe that they cannot function. Furthermore, panic attacks are not necessarily learned. Yes, we can learn more about what causes anxiety in ourselves, but the physical symptoms of panic attacks are more than simply learning to be fearful or anxious. At this time, scientists or clinicians know that there is a genetic correlation to panic attacks, but they have not identified the exact gene that causes them.

In one Mayo Clinic article about panic attacks and panic disorder, they state that clinicians may not know the exact cause of panic attacks, but they can predict the type of person that might experience a panic attack. People who are sensitive to stress can be prone to having panic attacks, along with those prone to negative emotions. Although the specific gene has not been identified, scientists have observed that certain changes in brain function may also make a person prone to anxiety attacks.

In the same article, it is pointed out that, as humans, we respond to impending danger with a **fight or flight response**. For example, when a rabid dog comes your way, you wouldn't stick around; you would run. During this reaction, you would experience an elevated heart rate and breathing that speeds up as you react to that life-threatening experience. However, with a panic attack, there isn't always impending, logical danger, despite the severe physical reactions that occur during the instance. In particular, a panic attack can be caused by something other people may hardly notice; for example, a noise or a strange smell could trigger an attack.

A person having a panic attack might not receive any warning that a panic attack is going to happen. You would know that when a rabid dog comes your way, you will have a naturally occurring fight or flight reaction, but what about if you are driving in your car and suddenly have a panic attack? There is nothing in the car that should make you nervous, and you are driving a route that you are very familiar with. Panic attacks can occur at any time and will continue to occur unless the individual can break the ongoing cycle.

Symptoms of a Panic Attack

You might not know when a panic attack will happen, but there are symptoms especially attributed to panic attacks. According to Mayo Clinic, the following is a list of symptoms that typically happen during a panic attack:

- A sense of impending doom or danger
- Chills
- Hot Flashes
- Nausea
- Abdominal cramping
- A sense of impending doom
- Sweating
- Fear of loss of control or death

- Rapid pounding heart rate
- Chest pain
- A feeling of unreality or detachment
- Numbness or tingling sensation
- Dizziness, lightheadedness, or faintness

If these symptoms weren't bad enough, there is also the fear of having another panic attack, as was mentioned in an earlier section. Consequently, you would begin to avoid situations that might cause a panic attack. You may not know exactly when or where you will have your next panic attack, so you begin to anticipate normal situations that *could* trigger you into having an attack.

You would also probably have to deal with unexpected triggers. You might react in panic to flashing lights or loud noises; however, although you learn to fear these situations, not all flashing lights or loud noises will make you have a panic attack.

As stated earlier, panic attacks are severe and unpleasant, generally causing the individual to try to avoid any situation that could cause them to have an attack. More and more the people who suffer from panic attacks withdraw from public life because they are scared of having an attack in public.

Psychological Symptoms and Reactions

We mentioned that panic attacks also have psychological symptoms, and the fear of death is very prominent in people suffering from attacks. Another psychological symptom of a panic attack is the fear of losing control, which can manifest to feelings of going crazy or losing one's mind. When a panic attack happens, you would feel like you have no control over the situation. Not knowing when a panic attack will happen or experiencing intense physical symptoms can make a person feel unsure about their sanity.

In the most severe cases, a person can experience a detachment of self and surroundings, which can cause a person to believe they are observing their life from outside their bodies (Mayo Clinic Staff, n.d.).

Panic Attacks and Other Disorders

There is not necessarily a specific medical test for panic attacks; however, doctors may test you to see if there are any medical reasons for your panic attacks or if you may have panic disorder. For example, if your heartbeat increases or you have chest pain, it could be related to panic attacks or something else, such as heart disease. When a doctor rules out a physical reason, they may send you to be evaluated by a psychologist or therapist. There, you would discuss the circumstances of your panic attacks.

Panic attacks may be part of another disorder that you are being treated for; specifically, you may have a social phobia or depression that may be causing you to experience attacks without warnings. Having depression or social phobia can make you more prone to having panic attacks, though remember that panic attacks can come about on their own without any pre-existing conditions.

If you have experienced a panic attack, there is no doubt that you need to ask for help, as panic attacks can carry severe symptoms with them, such as shortness of breath or chest pains. First, you must rule out a physical reason for these symptoms and, if you don't appear to have a physical reason for these symptoms, then you can explore whether they are caused by panic attacks.

Anticipatory Anxiety

Another way to tell that you are suffering from panic attacks is to evaluate your behavior between the attacks; during these times, you may be experiencing anticipatory anxiety or phobic avoidance, which will be important to notice.

According to Smith et al. (2019), anticipatory anxiety happens in between attacks. Instead of feeling calm and relaxed, you would have a sense of doom and feel tension and anxiety. Characteristics of anticipatory anxiety include the fear of having another panic attack. In this case, you would be constantly worried about having another panic attack, and such thoughts would manifest in the back of your mind.

Phobic avoidance happens when you avoid situations and places that could trigger your panic. This type of avoidance has two distinct characteristics: the first, as mentioned, being the avoidance of places where you think you would have another panic attack. For example, if you have panic attacks at your doctor's office before going through a procedure, you may begin to avoid visits in which procedures would be done. The second characteristic of phobic avoidance is when you avoid places where there is no easy escape; an example of this could be a family party or visiting your in-laws. In these situations, you feel trapped and like there is no escaping the social event. Plus, you would feel that if you had a panic attack, there would be no one there who could offer help.

You might be an anxious person who has a lot of anxiety, but remember that this fact does not necessarily mean you suffer from panic attacks; you might be only having anxiety attacks. When you have a panic attack, you are experiencing overwhelming fear about something, and your symptoms are generally scary and overwhelming.

The Traits of a Panic Attack

Remember that another trait of a panic attack is that they come about suddenly and without any obvious reason. With anxiety, you know the places that make you anxious, but with a panic attack, you would be feeling fine one minute, then experiencing overwhelming symptoms—which could include rapid heartbeat and nausea, for instance—the next.

The Diagnostic and Statistical Manual of Mental Disorders Fifth Edition (DSM-5) states that panic attacks are either unexpected or expected. Specifically, unexpected panic attacks happen without a foreseeable reason, whereas expected panic attacks happen because of triggers or known stressors in your environment, according to Vandergriendt (2019).

An example of having a panic attack and anxiety at the same time is like this: you worry about going to the doctor; you are restless and have a fear of losing control of yourself at the doctor's office. Then, when you arrive at the doctor's office, you feel chest pain, shortness of breath, sweating, chills, or hot flashes, and your heart rate is accelerated. This is a panic attack.

If you remain worried and apprehensive about the situation and those feelings increase when you go to the office, this is an *anxiety* attack. You feel terrible about being at the doctor's, but you can still pull through your visit on your own with relative coherence. It may be uncomfortable (and possibly more so than it would be for most people), but you should be able to stay for the visit and will feel better when it's over.

If you have a panic attack during the visit, you will likely be unable to go through with the visit at all, as your panic attack will require you to have assistance. You will feel the automatic fight or flight response, and you may even run out of the office and not stop running until you are a ways away from the office.

Panic Attack Triggers

Panic attacks are unexpected, but there may be triggers that cause panic attacks. These triggers might not be known to you, which is why the panic attack may seem like it is coming out of nowhere, according to Vandergriendt (2019).

Triggers for your panic attacks can be (but are not limited to) the following:

- A stressful job.
- Driving.
- Social situations.
- Phobias (such as agoraphobia or claustrophobia).
- Memories or reminders of a traumatic experience.
- Some physical situations/events that can cause panic attacks.
- Thyroid problems.
- Withdrawal from drugs or alcohol.
- Reaction to medication and supplements.
- Chronic illnesses such as asthma, irritable bowel syndrome, heart disease, and diabetes.

When you start receiving treatment, you may be able to see patterns in your behavior and begin to recognize your personal triggers.

Risk Factors

There are also risk factors for having a panic attack, as stated by Vandergriendt (2019).

Examples of these risk factors may include the following:

- Having an anxious personality.
- Drugs and alcohol use.
- Genetics—having a close family member with anxiety and/or panic disorder.
- Living with a life-threatening illness or a chronic health condition.
- Experiencing a stressful life event, such as death or divorce.
- Experiencing traumatic events when you were a child or as an adult.
- Ongoing stress and worries, like financial problems or family conflicts.

Learning to Deal with Your Panic Attacks

The good news about panic attacks is that you can receive treatment that will help you understand why you are having panic attacks and when you understand, you can begin to learn how to deal with them and eventually get them to stop happening. Furthermore, you can learn different techniques to battle those panic attacks. The purpose of this book is to help you understand your panic attacks better while learning specific techniques to help you combat them.

When working with a health professional, you can begin to identify triggers and even plan for what you are going to do when you have a panic attack. You can also share this book with your health professional, while your therapist can help you pick which techniques are best for you.

According to Vandergriendt (2019), before working with a mental health professional, your primary care physician (PCP) will want to give you a physical exam, blood test, or electrocardiogram (ECG or EKG). In fact, your PCP may have a questionnaire that will help them distinguish whether you are experiencing a physical or mental reaction during your panic attacks. When you are referred to a mental health practitioner, both you and the therapist will examine what you experience before a panic attack happens. This will help you to identify triggers that could cause you to have a panic attack. Also, your therapist will give you tools to cope with your panic attacks; for example, taking slow breaths or strategies to focus your attention elsewhere.

The Lasting Effects of a Panic Attack

Although very intense, a panic attack usually only lasts about ten minutes; however, the aftereffects of the panic attack can make a serious imprint on an individual's life and their psyche. Ongoing panic attacks can make a person feel like they are losing grip on reality. Intense panic attacks can cause an immense terror that may impact one's self-confidence, and this type of suffering often causes anticipatory anxiety or phobic avoidance.

The good news about panic attacks is that they can be treated with therapy and medication. There are also various techniques that you can use to help you make it through your panic attacks and, ultimately, help alleviate the intensity of your attacks.

Chapter Summary

There are many things to learn about panic attacks—they may occur due to trauma or another mental condition, such as bipolar disorder, social phobia, or depression.

- Mental health practitioners do not know what causes panic attacks.
- There are physical symptoms of panic attacks, such as shortness of breath and chest pain.
- There are psychological symptoms of panic attacks, such as fear of dying or losing control.

In the next chapter, you will learn about various myths and misconceptions about panic attacks.

CHAPTER THREE:

Myths and Misconceptions About Panic Attacks

Now that you are starting to better understand and notice the signs of your panic attacks, it is time to learn about the myths and misconceptions about them. Panic attacks are intense, and you might feel that you will die while having one. Your feelings may move beyond those of humiliation and fearing that you will lose control of your mental facilities. In this chapter, we will learn to recognize some of the things you might have been wondering about in terms of panic attacks and clear up any misconceptions you have.

With any condition, there are many myths and misconceptions that can make things worse; nevertheless, the more you know about panic attacks, the better you will feel. The following sections will detail these myths and misconceptions that people have about panic attacks and panic disorder.

Myth #1: Panic attacks are only a symptom of panic disorder.

Just because you have a panic attack, does not mean that you have panic disorder. A panic attack can still happen as a result of other types of disorders. Here is a list of disorders that can bring about a panic attack:

- Bipolar disorder
- Social anxiety disorder (SAD)
- Obsessive compulsive disorder (OCD)
- Generalized anxiety disorder (GAD)
- Specific phobias
- Irritable bowel syndrome (IBS)
- Various Digestive disorders
- Sleep disorders

Myth #2: Panic attacks are an overreaction to stress and anxiety.

Although feeling anxious due to stress and anxiety can be pretty intense, it isn't the same as having a panic attack. There are two important points to remember about panic attacks:

1. **A panic attack usually occurs without any warnings**. Before participating in therapy, some people who suffer from panic attacks usually have no idea why they had the attack. Unlike with an anxiety attack, when the person is stressed, they are not responding to immediate stress or anxiety; the panic attack just mysteriously happens. With therapy, a person can learn to identify triggers or environments that bring a panic attack to fruition, but it is seldom due to conditions they can control.

2. **People that have panic attacks do not have any control over what is happening**. A panic attack is very severe, and it is nothing like dealing with anxiety. A panic attack is more than having butterflies in your stomach; they are generally so intense that many people who suffer from them land in the emergency room.

Myth #3: Panic attacks can only occur when a person is awake.

Not all panic attacks happen when a person is awake. In fact, there is a name for panic attacks that happen especially at night: **nocturnal panic attacks**. Imagine sleeping, but right in the middle, you are jolted awake by the symptoms of a panic attack— shortness of breath or feeling that your heart is going to burst out of your chest all present during this nocturnal panic attack. Nocturnal attacks do not happen as often as daytime panic attacks, but they do occur.

When a person experiences a nocturnal panic attack, their sleep is disturbed and they often cannot go back to sleep. Nocturnal panic attacks bring with them feelings of fear and disconnection from yourself and your environment, and a nocturnal panic attack will often feel like they are part of a nightmare.

Myth #4: You can die from a panic attack.

The experience of a panic attack can be very intense, with some people experiencing major discomfort such as chest pains, accelerated heart rate, excessive sweating, chest pain, and shortness of breath during episodes. These symptoms often feel like a major physical event, such as a heart attack or something else just as serious happening to our lungs. Many experience symptoms fierce enough for them to have to head straight to the emergency room for treatment. In short, panic attack victims often feel like they are dying, and this fear is often the most prominent feeling during an attack.

However, no matter how intense the symptoms are, you will not die from a panic attack. The procedure in an emergency room is to stabilize and calm you down when you come in for treatment.

Some tests may be run to make sure that there is not a physical reason for your panic attack, but once the test comes back and indicates that you are physically healthy, the emergency room doctor will probably talk to you more so they can figure out if there were any other emergency problems that could have caused your panic attack.

There is often no apparent reason that you had a panic attack, and the absence of a reason should be a clue to your doctor. Not having a precondition to panic attacks is one of the major symptoms of an attack, and rest assured that a medical professional will know this.

Overall, there is no reason to fear that you will die from a panic attack.

Myth #5: Panic attacks can make you go insane.

Not having a warning that you are going to have a panic attack might make you feel out of control. Panic attacks usually last for ten minutes, with a peak before subsiding, and especially not knowing outright why you had that panic attack can make you believe you are losing control of yourself and in danger of going insane.

Yes, there might be underlying mental health reasons for having a panic attack, such as having suffered trauma and having problems dealing with that trauma; however, having panic attacks is not an indicator that you will lose control of your mental health.

The fear of completely losing control can become obsessive— you might feel that if you concentrate, you may be able to head off the panic attack. This is you trying to gain some control over what seems to be impossible to control, which is a major frustration that can go even further by making you feel helpless.

In this book, you will be presented with strategies you can use to cope with panic attacks. Panic attacks can make anyone feel humiliated, but there is hope that you will be able to become better at dealing with a panic attack when it happens—or better yet, even before it happens.

Overall, when panic strikes, rest assured that your sanity is intact and that, even if you lose control over yourself, it will only be for a brief period of time.

Myth #6: Panic attacks can be avoided.

When you start working on alleviating your panic attacks, you might discover what is triggering your attacks. This is a process of uncovering your feelings about the trauma you have experienced; however, there are many reasons you might be having panic attacks besides trauma. You could fear something with so much intensity that panic attacks happen every time you come near.

Yes, finding out what triggers your panic attacks goes a long way in alleviating and regaining control over them, but the truth is, even though you know your triggers and fears, panic attacks might still occur.

It is not healthy to think that if you avoid the things that cause you fear, you will avoid panic attacks. Avoiding your fears or staying away from what triggers you can become an impossible task. However, avoiding these things might just make your fears or triggers become even more intense.

The best way to experience a panic attack is to face them head-on and maintain a relaxed state. This book will go more in-depth about the strategies and things you can do to lessen the intensity of your panic attacks, which will also be much healthier ways of dealing with them, in contrast to trying to live a life where you restrict yourself and avoid potentially triggering situations.

Myth #7: There's little you can do about panic attacks.

After having more than one panic attack at a time, you might feel that there is no way out when it comes to having these attacks; however, you can work with a mental health professional to learn how to deal with these attacks and ultimately work to cease them altogether.

For you to begin the process of dealing therapeutically with your panic attacks, it is important that you find a mental health professional who can evaluate you and make a proper diagnosis. With that done, you can start treatment and, once you have your diagnosis, your doctor will likely be able to schedule you for psychotherapy, where you can discuss your panic attacks. Your doctor may also be able to prescribe medications that will help you better deal with your panic attacks and make it easier for you to participate in psychotherapy. Various medications will all target different areas in your brain and serve different purposes, so it is important to work closely with your doctor and decide which ones work best for you, whether that be antidepressants or medication that helps with anxiety.

Remember that no matter what treatment a doctor may prescribe, it is always important to make contact with a mental health professional first before taking medication.

Myth #8: You will be stuck with having panic attacks your whole life.

Although your panic attacks may feel epic, there are things you can do to lessen the intensity of the attack and ultimately stop having them altogether.

Medications and therapies like **cognitive behavioral therapy** (CBT) can go a long way in helping you conquer your panic attacks. In a later section, we will talk more about CBT and its effectiveness.

As it was stated in the previous section, a mental health professional is the first step to conquering your panic attacks; however, in the end, it will always be your motivation to work at therapy that will help you cease them in the end.

CBT therapy can be very successful, but you must put forth the effort to yield those successful results. Coming to terms with having panic attacks might be difficult at first, but the beginning step is to ask for help. When you receive the help you need, you will begin the process of alleviating the intensity of your panic attacks. You can use this book in conjunction with your therapy and the medication prescribed by your mental health professional.

Myth #9: Panic is a gateway to a more serious mental disorder.

Before you go see a mental health professional, you might believe that he or she is going to tell you that you are suffering from another type of disorder, such as bipolar disorder, schizophrenia, or even general anxiety.

The truth is that having panic attacks is a disorder in its own right; it is not any of the disorders mentioned above or any other kind of disorder that you have in mind. It is not a serious mental illness, but simply a condition where you experience panic or fear severely.

Panic attacks can be treated, and you will be able to cut down on the intensity of your panic attacks with a lot of dedicated work in therapy, while also being diligent about taking your medication.

Myth #10: Loved ones cannot help you with your panic attacks.

Panic attacks are very personal, and you might feel so humiliated by them that you don't want to tell anyone about your episodes; however, this does not have to be the case. As you work with your therapist, you might want to include other people in your close circle with the information you are learning in therapy.

It isn't necessary to tell the world, but the more you explain to others, the better you will feel. Perhaps someone you are close to can add some insight into why you are having panic attacks in the first place.

The people who care about you are worried, so perhaps you might consider giving them information that can help them feel involved in assisting you through your therapeutic journey. Yet, if you are a private person, and telling others might disrupt the progress of your therapy, that is all right too. You are always in control of the information you want to reveal to others.

Now that we have busted some of the myths and your preconceived notions about panic attacks, you are ready to start learning some effective strategies to combat panic attacks.

Furthermore, this book will be providing powerful techniques and tools that you can use to help deal with your panic attacks.

Chapter Summary

There are many misconceptions about panic attacks, and in this chapter, we discussed ten. Here are three of the main myths that we covered:

- Panic attacks are not the only symptom of panic disorder.
- You can die from a panic attack.
- There's little you can do to lessen the intensity of a panic attack.

These myths and misconceptions might appear scary and intimidating, and can also make panic attacks appear overwhelming, incurable, and uncontrollable. The truth is that panic attacks *are* treatable. You can learn techniques that will help you to deal with your panic attack, including attending therapy and asking your doctor about available medication that can help alleviate your symptoms.

In the next chapter, you will learn how the five steps of AWARE that can help calm you down during an intense panic attack.

CHAPTER FOUR:

How to Feel Calm During an Intense Panic Attack

The possibility of being unable to control a panic attack may seem upsetting to anyone suffering. True, you can study patterns and triggers that happen before a panic attack, but these attacks will still happen no matter how much information you learn unless you know how to combat them.

Don't feel bad because there is something you can do during your panic attacks that will make the situation better. You can learn to be calm and accepting of your panic attacks.

In this chapter, we will discuss the five steps of AWARE:

1. Acknowledge and Accept
2. Wait and Watch (Work)
3. Actions (that make you more comfortable)
4. Repeat
5. End

According to Barends Psychology Practice (n.d.), the first of the five steps of AWARE is to acknowledge and accept what is happening during the panic attack. It is even possible to stop the panic attack with AWARE, but no matter what, the first thing that you still must do is acknowledge and accept your anxiety.

Right before you have a panic attack, you might be experiencing fear; then, the panic attack starts and you are practically bathed in fear. This is okay. It is important to acknowledge the fear and to remind yourself that you are not in any specific danger. The feeling of being in danger is a symptom of a panic attack, but remember that this is just a thought—it is neither true nor relevant. Go with that fear and don't pretend that it is not happening; once you go with the fear, you are ready for the first part of AWARE: Accept.

Accepting Your Panic Attack

When you accept the symptoms of your panic disorder, you are on your way to lessening the intensity of your panic attacks. Remember that you are not in any physical danger, but merely experiencing a fear that can be put back into your control.

Another component to AWARE is that when you are experiencing a panic attack, you are experiencing the worst that is going to happen; nothing else coming your way will be worse than your current situation. Take a moment to ride the panic attack to its ending (Carbonell, 2020).

Resisting the panic attack will only make it worse. If you just acknowledge and accept that a panic attack is happening to you, on the other hand, you will cut down on the intensity of the attack.

Waiting

The next step of AWARE is wait. When you have a panic attack, you probably experience the need to flee or struggle.

However, rash action will only make things worse. So often when you have a panic attack, you are reduced to a state in which you cannot think straight and are more prone to do something rash. Moreover, you will make decisions that can just make your circumstance worse.

This is the time to *wait*, as it will lessen your attack's intensity the longer you do so. If you run away from the task or do something to escape the panic attack, you will deprive your subconscious of recognizing that your panic attack has a beginning and an end.

If you take a moment to wait and watch, you will find some relief, and the feelings that you are having at that time will start to die down. In fact, you might even be able to think clearer.

Watch

The next thing you want to do is watch. This is when you take a moment to see how your panic attack is working. It is important to take note of and observe the happenings before your panic attack, as well as during, at this time. By observing these actions, you gain the opportunity to work on a panic diary for taking notes about important details of your panic attacks.

Imagine that, during a panic attack, you wait and watch by writing into your panic diary. This can be a small notebook or an attractive journal that you carry with you at all times. By writing in your panic diary, you gain the chance to calm down and be distracted from the intensity of the panic attack.

When you fill out a panic diary, you are moving from being a victim to an observer. If it is not possible to write in a diary, find another way to become an observer; you can use a smartphone app that will let you record voice memos, or a tablet or other device that you can use to create a panic diary.

Work

You can also add "work" to this step. When you are having an anxiety attack, you may be unable to wait and watch immediately; this is where "work" comes in. For example, you might be driving your car or giving a presentation. Don't freak out and run from this event, but instead, remain engaged in what you are doing and move calmly toward watching and waiting while you are having your panic attack.

I know that this may sound difficult, but let's walk through a scenario. Let's say you are driving your car and you begin to have the symptoms of a panic attack. Your heart feels like it is going to burst through your chest; your breathing starts to come rapidly, and you begin to feel nauseous. When this happens, you are unable to pull to the side of the road because there is no safe place for you to park and wait. You could keep driving, but while in the act, "watch" the panic attack and wait for it to end. Observe how you are feeling, follow the intensity, and know that the panic attack will end, as it will not go on for an infinite amount of time. Remember—you are an observer, not a victim.

Finding Calm During a Panic Attack

What can you do during your panic attack? We've already established that you shouldn't do anything rash; it is important for you to watch and wait.

It is easy to panic and think that your panic attack will never end, but what is it that you already know about panic attacks? Do they indeed last forever? If they did, you would not be reading this book. It is a certainty of life that panic attacks do end.

So, what do you do when a panic attack happens? Well, your job is to make yourself more comfortable with the attack. Carbonell (2020) suggests some techniques that have been helpful to people suffering from panic attacks:

- Belly breathing or diaphragmatic breathing.
- Talking yourself through the attack.
- Getting involved with your present.
- Working with your body.

These techniques are not so hard to do. Belly breathing is as easy as taking a deep breath to fill your belly, then letting the breath back out slowly.

Talking to yourself silently or aloud can reinforce the idea that your panic attack is not going to last forever. You can tell yourself that it is okay to be afraid or that this incident will help you observe your panic attacks' characteristics, so you can learn to be more of an observer than a victim.

Getting involved with your present is important. If you are in the middle of an activity, start concentrating on the present and tasks that you have to accomplish. For example, if you are about to start a presentation, or you are in the middle of the presentation, get involved in your notes or on the slides you are projecting. It's almost like making your world stop spinning so you can carry on with what you are doing—even though you are experiencing a panic attack.

Working towards being aware of your body, can relax the tense areas of your body. Concentrate on the parts of your body that are tense and work to relieve that tension. Loosen up that rigidity in your body and release any tense muscles. Also, don't hold your breath during a panic attack; concentrate on your belly breathing instead.

Overall, you must attend to and take care of yourself, so you feel more comfortable during a panic attack, thus alleviating your symptoms. It can be done. Don't be a victim, but get actively involved in making yourself more comfortable with your situation.

If you need a visual, think of a time you saw a nurse make a patient in her care more comfortable when that patient was sick and worried. To help more with your situation in the long run, work on helping the caregiver inside of you.

Repeat

Sometimes panic attacks have several cycles. You might have just gone through the five steps of AWARE, then another cycle begins again. Don't despair and believe that you have failed—it is just the nature of a panic attack to come in waves. Having a panic attack might feel like waves crashing into you, and if you flail around in the water, you will lose control and expose yourself to the danger of drowning. However, if you keep your wits about you, you can survive the attack waves of a panic attack.

When you find yourself entering a new cycle of an intense panic attack, keep your wits about you and start the AWARE cycle. It might be hard for you to do, but if you acknowledge and accept that you are having a longer panic attack, you will be able to wait and watch (and possibly continue on with your work). Then, you can get into *action* and make yourself more comfortable until the panic attack eventually ends.

End

The final step of awareness is to end the panic attack.

Don't be frightened if you have to start all over two or more times. Remember that you are keeping a panic diary, so you are an observer and not a victim.

Even though you might have several cycles in your panic attack, they do end eventually. Rest assured that your whole life won't become one constant, chronic panic attack. Invest in the five steps of AWARE so the panic attacks become less intense.

It is not your job to make the attack end—your job is to make the five steps of AWARE happen. Let's review the steps of AWARE:

1. Acknowledge and Accept
2. Wait and Watch (and/or Work)
3. Actions (that make you comfortable)
4. Repeat
5. End

When your panic attack ends, you might feel shaken up and uncertain of yourself. As has been reiterated multiple times, panic attacks are very intense, and even if you did the five steps of AWARE, you still lived through yet another episode of panic. At this time, you have some choices in your thinking: you could feel a sense of doom that you can't predict when a panic attack happens. You might even believe that, no matter what you do, you will have to live through a panic attack yet again until whatever you are doing for therapy (be it medications, counseling, CBT) takes effect.

This is your chance to step up and have a positive attitude, like expecting the best. Review your panic diary information, and you will see that, little by little, your reactions to your panic attacks will be improving. Praise yourself for becoming an observer rather than a victim.

Being AWARE

It may never have occurred to you that you could be more aware during a panic attack. People who experience panic attacks often feel a sense of doom in their existence. In fact, sometimes the panic attacks seem like they will only feel worse as time goes on.

Learning and doing the five steps of AWARE can be the answer that will lift you up. Banish that feeling of doom by studying these steps closely and enacting them when a panic attack hits you.

Make sure to work on filling out a panic diary, whether it is in a notebook or on a smart device, as you will be writing down some very important data. This data can be shown to your mental health provider, and both of you can study what is going on when you have your attacks. It can be very helpful to your provider to know what you are experiencing.

There are still even more techniques in this book that can help you. Keep the faith and know that help is on the way.

Chapter Summary

Using the five steps of AWARE will help you remain calm during a panic attack, and staying calm during a panic attack can help lessen the intense symptoms you would experience in a panic attack. The five steps of AWARE are the following:

1. Acknowledge and Accept
2. Wait and Watch (or Work)
3. Actions (That make you more comfortable)
4. Repeat
5. End

These five steps will help you alleviate your panic attacks. Being aware and accepting your panic attacks might be the most difficult thing to do, but it can go a long way in helping you deal with your panic attacks. Often, there is more than one cycle of panic attacks, so it is best to repeat the five steps until your panic attack ends.

In the next chapter, you will learn how to stop your panic attacks.

CHAPTER FIVE:

How to Stop Panic Attacks

Once you have learned the five steps of AWARE and have mastered them, you can look at trying some new techniques that can help stop your panic attacks completely. It is very important to accept and recognize your panic attacks; however, learning to focus on something other than your panic attack can also be beneficial.

In this chapter, you will learn twelve different techniques that you can use to stop your panic attacks. At first, doing some of these things while experiencing a panic attack may be difficult, but with a little practice, implementing them is achievable. You might want to try practicing these techniques and getting good at using them, so when you do have a panic attack, it will be easier to take action.

Teach Yourself to Focus

Although you might feel that it is impossible to do anything but feel terror during a panic attack, it is still possible to do something to quell the attack, despite these feelings. The best thing to do is to teach yourself to focus and act specifically to break your concentration away from the attack.

In the last chapter, we discussed how important it is to accept and recognize that you are having a panic attack. Being able to stop, accept, and recognize that the panic attack can go a long way to actually cutting down the duration of your attack.

It is very important that you don't fight the panic attack or get over-excited. If you are calm and accept that you are having an attack, there is a chance that the symptoms of the panic attack will be less intense than they could be.

Panic Attacks Don't Last Forever

This was mentioned earlier, but to reiterate—if you give recognition to the fact that this panic attack is not going to last forever and that the panic attack will stop at some point in time, you *can* defeat that overwhelming fear that your panic attack will never end. Though panic attacks can be quite overwhelming at times, remember that you are experiencing just a short period of concentrated anxiety.

Physical Symptoms

There may be times that your symptoms feel more physical than mental. Perhaps you just had your first panic attack and you are not sure of its cause. It is good to get a checkup and visit with your doctor to see if there are any physical reasons you might be having intense symptoms like tightening of the chest or excessive sweating and heart palpitations.

Asking for Help

It may also be helpful to talk to your doctor about finding a good psychiatrist or therapist, as they may be able to refer you to other mental health professionals whom they would have a working relationship with. In this way, you will have a team that can work out a unique and effective care plan for you.

Controlling Your Breath

It is possible that your panic attack will take your breath away in its intensity. You may start to breathe rapidly and feel like you can't catch your breath. On occasion, this type of breathing can also make your chest feel tight. When this happens, you can do something that will help you make these symptoms less intense.

Deep breathing and counting slowly to four while you are breathing in and out can be a great help. Continuing to breathe rapidly instead may increase your anxiety and cause extreme tension in your body, eventually resulting in other physical symptoms, like a tight chest or a heavyweight feeling on your chest. Therefore, it is important to concentrate on controlling your breathing.

Breathe deeply, like you are filling up a balloon, and count slowly as you expand your lungs. Breathing in this manner can help you concentrate on something else besides your panic attack. This concentration can then help you get through the panic attack.

Deep breathing is something to focus on, so you can believe internally that you can survive the attack. Moreover, deep breathing can help you feel more in control of the situation and add to your comfort level during a panic attack. Specifically, it is very effective to have something else to focus on during a panic attack.

Medications for Your Panic Attack

We will discuss various other techniques to help you during an attack, but something to consider is taking medications to help quell your attacks. If you're being treated by a psychiatrist or your primary caregiver, you may be prescribed medication to help you get through the intensity of a panic attack. This medication may be prescribed to take regularly in the morning, night, or during the day. Moreover, you may be given medicines to take pro re nata (PRN). A medication that is considered PRN means you would take that medication when you need it.

If you have been prescribed a PRN medication, it is important to have it close by, so when you have a panic attack, you are able to take it. A PRN medication may be able to cut the duration and intensity of the panic attack significantly if you take it properly.

Some PRN medications you may be prescribed include beta-blockers or a benzodiazepine. Propranolol is a popular beta-blocker that is prescribed to help lower a racing heartbeat and decrease blood pressure.

Benzodiazepines like Valium, Xanax, or Klonopin can help calm you down, but you need to be cautious when taking this kind of medication because it is highly addictive. Your body can also gain a tolerance the more of this medication you take. However, benzodiazepines are still very effective in treating anxiety and panic attacks. Remember to use caution when taking this medication, and only take it when it is prescribed by your doctor.

Medications can be great for helping you control your panic attacks, but being careful to choose surroundings that will not trigger your panic attacks is just as important. A more comprehensive list of medications that treat anxiety can be found in Chapter 7.

Bombarding Your Senses

In an ever-changing, fast-paced world, there are a lot of things that can bombard and overload our senses. Loud music is something that everyone has to deal with time and again when going out for a night on the town, or even during a dining experience at a restaurant. Furthermore, there are instances when lights will bombard you. Many popular bars and grills have installed extremely large television screens for their patrons. These television screens may show everything from football games, to popular television shows or special events. Some restaurants have more than one screen on the wall.

When you are bombarded by a lot of stimuli, your brain may react negatively, and it is not unusual for these stimuli to overwhelm your senses and cause a panic attack. Pay attention to warning signs that are posted to warn patrons about flashing lights. Some movies even come with a warning posted at the box office that tells the patron there will be a lot of overwhelming stimuli (flashing lights) during the movie.

If you have panic attacks due to overwhelming stimuli, it is important that you learn to stay away from bright light and sounds. If you can't prevent your exposure and find that bright lights are triggering your panic attack, try to remove yourself from the central area of the noise. If this isn't an option, find a spot in the room where your exposure is limited and do your best to focus on your breathing or any other action that you think can help you get through and/or alleviate the symptoms of your panic attack.

Panic Attacks and Triggers

A "trigger" is something that causes or influences an event or situation to occur—in this case, a panic attack. It is not known for sure what specific events would bring about a panic attack, as we do not conclusively know what causes a panic attack. However, patients have reported that they have panic attacks after being exposed to specific things, such as bright lights, loud noises, enclosed spaces, and crowds. How do you become aware of the triggers that may be causing your panic attacks? One thing you could always do is keep a journal or a diary about the events that trigger your panic attacks.

By keeping a diary about your panic attacks, you might find patterns or indications that certain situations are causing your panic attacks. Until you can work through these situations with your therapist, it is wise to be aware of the things that trigger you. However, do not go to the extreme of staying at home or not participating in an event because you may be exposed to one of your triggers. In therapy, you can work toward desensitizing yourself to the situations that come before you have a panic attack. It is important that you learn about your triggers and actively work toward dealing with them healthily.

Exercising to Release Endorphins

Another healthy way to deal with an anxiety attack is light exercise. Even though there is no way to prepare for a panic attack, exercising is something that will make you feel better.

Exercise is more than just toning your body and burning calories; it helps release endorphins that can improve your mood and relax your body. When you do something as simple as walking, you release these endorphins into your system. Furthermore, walking can help you deal with a stressful environment. A short walk during a stressful time can help you with regulating your breathing and releasing any nervous tension that has built up when you are stressed.

Walking during a panic attack can help you focus on something other than what is causing the panic. It can also help with alleviating your fight or flight instincts. To summarize, there are many benefits of light exercise when you are having to cope with panic attacks.

Getting exercise is very important for your physical wellbeing, but being mindful can also contribute to reducing the effects of an intensive panic attack. When having a panic attack, it is important to stay focused, even though you are having intense physical reactions. Being mindful can help stop a panic attack.

Being Mindful

Mindfulness is the state of being aware or conscious of what is happening around you. Being mindful will help you deal with the present. Once you are more aware of the present, you can accept that you are having a panic attack, and noticing your bodily sensations, thoughts, and feelings will help you with your recovery.

Niemiec (2017) states that mindfulness is paying attention on purpose. Sometimes, when you have a panic attack, you might get the feeling that you are detached from reality. However, there are exercises you can do while having a panic attack that can bring you back to yourself. Some examples of these exercises include the following:

1. Listen for four distinct sounds and think of why they are all different from each other.
2. Pull your attention to five different things around you and pay attention to why each one is different from the other.
3. Choose three objects and describe to yourself how they are all different, such as in texture, use, and temperature.

4. Focus on one or two different smells around you. What are they and have you smelled them before?
5. Taste something: a candy that you carry in your pocket or purse for example.

Doing exercises such as these will pull your focus away from the panic attack and bring you into the present, which is exactly what you want.

Focusing on One Object

Being mindful is a good way to stay in the present and focus. However, it might be hard, at first, to be mindful without a little bit of practice. One thing you can do to become good at being mindful is to master the art of focusing on one object.

This simple task can really help you while you are having a panic attack. Pick one object near you and focus on it completely. Study that object and determine its qualities to help you focus. What color is the shape? What texture is it? Questions like this can help you tune in to that focus.

You can even carry something with you that you can focus on when you think a trigger or overload of stimuli will appear. A polished rock or crystal can be easy to put in your pocket and will count as a good thing to focus on when a panic attack happens. Doing this might take you out of the chaos that hits when you have an anxiety attack.

When you are having a panic attack, your muscles might tense up. Along with focusing on an object, you can also focus on letting go of the tension in your muscles. Progressive Muscle Relaxation (PMR) might be a good exercise to try while in the midst of a panic attack.

Muscle Relaxation

The key to this exercise is to slow down your breathing and give yourself permission to relax. When you are calm, your breathing will slow down and you can begin to concentrate on your muscle groups and tell yourself mentally to relax. This exercise, or PMR, is simply focusing on each set of muscles in your body and visualizing the muscles relaxing.

There are many different muscle groups that you can focus on—though there may be quite a few groups to remember, some good places to start include focusing on your arms, then your head, neck, shoulders, chest, then hips, and, lastly, your legs and your feet. One by one, tense these muscle groups and feel that tension for 5 seconds, then release your muscles and relax for ten seconds. Do this with your whole body. PMR has a two-fold purpose: first, it gives you something to focus on, and second, you can relax the muscles that have likely become very tense during your panic attack.

Find Your Happy Place

In everyone's experience, there is a place where we are happy and at our best. Perhaps it is a bench in a beautiful park or somewhere at the beach. Each person has their very own happy place.

If it is hard for you to focus on something in the room, close your eyes and bring your happy place into your vision. Take a moment to think about how you feel when you are in this location; think of as many details as you can think of and completely focus on this happy place.

When you think about a calm environment and a place that brings you true happiness, it becomes harder for your panic attack to continue.

Finding a Mantra

A mantra is a word, phrase, or sound that can help you focus (Crawford, 2018). For example, I like to think of the word "happy" when I am stressed. You may have a word or phrase that makes you happy, such as "there's no place like home."

By chanting this mantra, you are taking your mind off the panic attack and thinking and doing something positive for yourself. Another good phrase that you can use during a panic attack is "This too shall pass." This specific mantra not only takes your focus off your panic attack, but it also gives you confidence that what you are going through will end eventually, and that it cannot last forever.

When you find your mantra, try it and see how it helps you regulate your breathing and relax your muscles. This is a good step to stopping your panic attacks, as it not only helps you relax, but a good mantra can also soothe you and help take the anxiety away.

Finding Help During Your Panic Attacks

When you are experiencing a panic attack, it is good to have some help. Perhaps you have a spouse or a friend whom you can tell about these panic attacks. Pick an important person in your life to help you with a panic attack when it occurs.

This person might be like a coach who helps you get through a tough spot by reminding you to do the techniques that can help you when you are having a rough time. For example, you can tell this person to remind you to focus, or you can make this person familiar with muscle relaxation techniques, and they can help you go through that routine.

If you are having a panic attack in a public place, it is still possible to ask for help from the people around you. With your best effort, ask a person to take you to a secluded spot where you can concentrate more on how you can stop your panic attack. Whether in public or in private, it is good to have some help while going through a panic attack.

Panic attacks can be a major intrusion. They can be terrifying and make you feel like the world is crashing down around you. That is why it is important to learn how to stop your panic attacks. You can use one or several things listed in this chapter to help you stop your panic attack when it happens. In particular, it is important for you to believe that you have some input in a situation that initially feels out of control. Memorize these strategies for stopping your panic attacks, so when you do have an attack, you are ready to alleviate it quickly.

Chapter Summary

In this chapter, you learned how to stop panic attacks. Along with using the steps from AWARE, it is important to do things that will help you end the panic attack. The following list outlines the strategies outlined in this chapter that you can take to stop a panic attack:

- Deep breathing.
- Take your medication (if prescribed).
- Limit stimuli.
- Know your triggers.
- Perform light, rhythmic exercise.

- Do mindfulness exercises.
- Focus on something.
- Try muscle relaxation techniques.
- Picture your happy place.
- Repeat a mantra.
- Ask people you trust for help.

Doing these steps along with accepting and recognizing your panic attacks, you will be able to successfully stop your panic attacks from taking over your life.

In the next chapter, you will learn more about some powerful relaxation techniques.

CHAPTER SIX:

Powerful Relaxation Techniques

Going through this book, you are learning new techniques to help you when you are having a panic attack. Some of the techniques presented may get repeated, though it is not because there is a shortage of techniques to employ—it is just that some techniques are worth mentioning twice.

Techniques that help you through your panic attack can be as simple as counting or as complex as mindfulness. Learn as many techniques as possible and don't be afraid to add some techniques of your own.

Practicing these techniques is very important. In order to successfully use these strategies, work on doing them while you are not having a panic attack. Try one at a time and, once you master a technique, move on to the next one until you have a repertoire of techniques you can use when you have a panic attack.

Thoughtful Relaxation Can Make a Difference

When you are having a panic attack, your entire body is tensed up. The fear during a panic attack will put your body on the alert for some kind of danger. Adrenaline is released and your muscles tense. Trying to relax is, thus, *crucial* during a panic attack.

Although you can't anticipate when a panic attack is going to happen, you can prepare for one by learning different techniques. Relaxation during a panic attack is very important. You do more harm than good when you tense up and get very anxious. In fact, the higher the degree of tension in your body, the more intense a panic attack will be.

However, if you learn some relaxation techniques, you can curb the intensity and, hopefully, your reaction to the panic attack will be tamer than if you started out tense before the attack. These relaxation techniques work because they address your body's stress responses, such as an increased heart rate, rapid breathing, and tense muscles.

If you take the time to practice some relaxation techniques, you can be ready for when a panic attack begins.

Breathing Techniques

When you experience a panic attack, your breathing becomes an issue; either you are taking shallow breaths or breathing very fast. Consequently, learning to relax your breathing can go a long way in toning down the intense body reactions you are having during a panic attack.

To get your breathing under control when you are anxious, you might want to follow these steps:

- Ask someone to find you a quiet and comfortable place for you to sit while you are experiencing your panic attack.
- When you are seated at the quiet spot, put one hand on your stomach and the other on your chest, then breathe deeply.

For example, you can inhale and imagine your abdomen filling up with air, like a balloon.

- Take a slow and regular breath, in through your nose. Watch and sense your hands as you breathe in. The hand on your chest should remain still while the hand on your stomach will move slightly.
- Breathe out through your mouth slowly.
- Repeat this process at least ten times, or until you begin to feel your anxiety quiet down.

Another breathing technique is to let our thumb and your middle finger pinch your nostrils shut. Lift your middle finger and breathe in, watching the hand on your stomach move. Hold your breath and let your middle finger close your nostril once again. Now it's the thumbs turn to lift up. Exhale the air you are holding through this open nostril. When you are finished with that, start the process again for as long as it takes for you to feel better. This type of breathing is popular in yoga meditation.

Using Thoughts About Your Happy Place

In the last chapter, we talked about finding your happy place during a panic attack and focusing on that place. This technique is successful because it helps to relax your brain and body. The place you are thinking of can be real or imaginary; it just has to be a place that makes you happy and relaxed. Don't make it so complicated that reproducing it in your mind causes anxiety within you.

When you are having a panic attack, it is important for you to slow your relative time as much as possible. When thinking about your happy place, reflect on the details that require you to focus. Remembering that pondering how a place smells, sounds, and feels is a simple way of getting yourself to refocus. You don't necessarily have to remember very specific details about your happy place, such as the exact number of stairs up from the beach to the patio or the color of the walls down to the shade. Just keep it simple.

When you've thought of the details of your happy place, concentrate on being there in your mind. Take slow breaths through your nose and mouth, and focus on your breathing and the details of your happy place. Continue to do this until the panic attack starts to go away.

Positive Thoughts and Their Power

While in the midst of a panic attack, you might be experiencing a lot of negative or anxious thoughts. Sometimes the great intensity of a panic attack makes the sufferer believe they are going to die. Your thoughts might spiral downward into imagining the worst possible outcomes. Therefore, it is important to interrupt these anxious thoughts and stop them from taking over and increasing the harm from your panic attack.

The first thing you can do is become aware that your thoughts are making you anxious. Then, you must interrupt those negative thoughts and place some more positive thinking into your head, so you can stop or interrupt the negative. Some techniques that you might want to try include the following:

- Think of a person you love and remember the details or qualities that make you love that person.
- Think of something you look forward to doing in the future, like going out to a movie or a great restaurant.
- Carry your favorite book with you, so you can take it out to read when you feel a panic attack beginning.

- Turn on the radio or use your smartphone to play music that makes you happy.
- If you were doing something important during the panic attack, try to go back to it and focus completely on what you were doing.

Use these techniques to interrupt the thinking that makes your panic attack worse. It is important for you to shift your attention away from your anxiety and into something positive that can pull you away from the panic attack's intensity.

Using Mindfulness to Live in the Present

As discussed in the last chapter, practicing mindfulness can be very rewarding. Practice being mindful before you have a panic attack, so it can become second nature to you. To practice mindfulness, you need to do the following things (Legg, 2018):

- Take yourself to a quiet and pleasant place to be. Sit down and close your eyes.
- Concentrate on your breathing and how your body feels.
- Shift your focus from your breathing and body, and begin to pay attention to what is around you. Pay attention to what you hear, feel, and smell. Ask yourself, "What is going on around me?"
- Continue to be mindful and switch back and forth from focusing on your body and focusing on what is going on around you until the anxiety begins to fade.

Mindfulness is the best way to bring yourself back to the present. It is also a very important tool to use when you are having a panic attack. Mindfulness is about achieving a calm state and extinguishing the rapid-fire negative thinking that goes on during a panic attack. When you are mindful, you are living in the present, and when you live in the present, there is no past or future to worry about—only the present would mean anything to you.

Releasing Tension

In the last chapter, we discussed how it is important to relax your muscles. Doing PMR is a great way to release tension; however, there is also another technique you can try while you are having a panic attack.

1. Find a comfortable place to be, then close your eyes and focus on your breathing. Inhale slowly through your nose, then exhale through your mouth.
2. Make a tight fist and squeeze your hand as hard as you can.
3. Hold the fist for a few seconds and think of the tension in your hand.
4. Open your hand slowly and notice the tension leaving your hand. Feel your hand getting lighter as you relax.
5. Try this technique on other parts of your body like your legs, shoulders, and feet.

If there is any place on your body that is injured, stay away from it during this muscle relaxation technique. The good thing about this technique is that you can choose how far you take it—if you are having trouble concentrating, try to do as much as you can. Repeat the same areas if you need to. The most important thing is that you are shifting your focus away from the panic attack and experiencing some relaxation.

A Simple Technique

One of the easiest things you can do when you are having a panic attack is count. When the panic attack starts, move yourself to a quiet and safe place. If you are doing something like driving or walking in a crowd, take yourself to the side of the road or somewhere safe to sit. Once you are in that safe place, close your eyes and begin counting to 10. It might be hard to focus on doing it during a panic attack, but be patient with yourself and keep trying to count. Once you have reached 10, try to get to 20 and so on, until your anxiety goes away.

If you can't close your eyes, you can still count. Just keep doing the task and count as much as you can, or count the same numbers over and over. Along with counting, don't forget to breathe.

Other Techniques to Consider

Take care of your stress levels

The techniques covered in this chapter can also be done when you are *not* experiencing a panic attack. There are often times when we feel really stressed. If you take care of that stress with one of these techniques, you may be able to lower your stress levels, and, perhaps, you might even be able to avoid a high enough stress level that would bring about a panic attack.

Avoid the triggers you know about

After a while, you may notice patterns form after having a few panic attacks. If you are in therapy, discuss these patterns. If you are not in therapy, rely on your panic diary for forming conclusions about what can be triggering your attacks.

There is a fine line between avoiding things that trigger you and withdrawing yourself from your usual routine. Be cautious of how you choose to remove yourself from situations that trigger your panic attacks. It can be as simple as choosing seats at a concert that are away from the bright lights and crowds. Sitting on the balcony when possible can take you away from your triggers without preventing you from staying away from the concert.

Make a plan

Pick a friend or a family member to help you when you have a panic attack. Have a plan that is especially for them when you are having a panic attack. For example, you can have them take you to a quiet and secure place. You can also teach this person a deep breathing technique that can help you lower the intensity of your panic attack, and discuss whether or not this person should consider taking you to the ER and under which circumstances. Overall, it is important to have a plan that you can share with a person whom you trust.

Social support

Everyone experiences stressful situations. Don't be afraid to explain to the people in your social circle that you are experiencing panic attacks—you would be surprised to learn how many people actually understand your situation. The more support you have around you, the better the chance that there will be someone around to help you when you are having an episode.

Being proactive

Even though panic attacks happen when you least expect it, you can be proactive and practice the techniques given in this chapter. It can be hard to get through a panic attack, but these techniques might make it easier.

If you think of a technique that has not been mentioned here, by all means, still try it. There are many strategies that have not been mentioned in this chapter that can help you feel better, such as acupressure or listening to nature sounds. Take this chapter as a sample of what is out there for you to try.

Every panic attack is unique, and you might have to try different techniques until you find one that really works. Review these techniques with your therapist and practice them when you can. Don't let a panic attack pull you away from friends and family who can help you; in fact, ask for help whenever possible.

Chapter Summary

In this chapter, you learned about powerful relaxation techniques that you can do during a panic attack. It is important to respond to your body's stress; you can lower your heart rate, stop your rapid breathing, and tense your muscles by doing the techniques described in this chapter.

- It is important for you to keep your breathing under control while having a panic attack.
- Visualize your happy place during a panic attack.
- Interrupt your anxious thought cycle.
- Practice mindfulness.

In the next chapter, you will learn about preventing your panic attacks.

CHAPTER SEVEN:

How to Prevent Panic Attacks

Despite the current research, we still are not sure why panic attacks happen. Is it a brain thing? Does it have to do with stress? Does it have to do with trauma? It is hard to know the answer to these questions because mental health professionals have yet to find the origin behind panic attacks. Just because we don't know the cause of panic attacks doesn't mean that we can't try techniques that will help lessen our chances of a panic attack. In this chapter, we will look at preventative techniques that you can do on your own.

Conquering Stress

The first thing that you must do to help prevent a panic attack is to take care of yourself. Whether it is getting a good night's sleep or eating a balanced diet, it is important that you do everything you can to remain healthy and strong.

Stress is believed to be a factor that can make a panic attack stronger. Even if you have a panic attack, if you are managing your stress well, you can weaken the panic attack's intensity because you are calm, to begin with.

To be able to withdraw stress as a factor, work on the stressors that you have in your life and break them down to smaller nuggets that can't overwhelm you. Get enough sleep and rest, so you can be strong enough to handle your stress.

Learn to practice meditation or do relaxation techniques. These techniques can go a long way in helping you when you are having a stressful day. Keeping a journal about your challenges can also help with stress. By writing about your stressors, you can work out a better plan for dealing with them.

Strategies to Relieve Stress

Regular exercise can also help you work off some of that stress. Even if it is only 15-20 minutes a day, any type of physical activity can help you release some of the stress that is manifesting itself.

As mentioned in the previous section, another thing you can do to deal with stress is to get enough sleep. If you are staying up late and waking up early, you will feel a deficit of rest that will weaken your ability to deal with challenges. Sleep is *so* important to your wellbeing; in fact, if you are having trouble getting a good night's rest, it might be good to schedule an appointment with your primary care physician to talk about your inability to sleep.

Overall, being able to be well-rested and calm about your challenges will help you avoid severe panic attacks.

A Healthy Diet Will Do You Good

While preventing panic attacks, you need to consider your diet. The food you eat is important—a diet rich in whole grains, vegetables, and fruit can help you feel full and well-fed. Processed foods won't go a long way in satisfying your appetite, nor will a diet that is mainly carbohydrates. The problem is that you may have a drop in your blood sugar, which would make you feel weak. Another important thing to note about nutrition is that you should be eating three solid meals a day, along with snacks. Your body needs to be nourished. If you are feeling jittery or massively hungry, you might be more prone to panic attacks. Maintaining a healthy and nourishing eating routine can help make you feel better.

It is also wise to drink enough water to stay hydrated, and have limited access to or avoiding caffeine altogether. Your body needs to stay hydrated to function well. Also, the over-consumption of alcohol is another thing to watch while maintaining a good diet. Alcohol can spike your blood levels and create havoc for your body.

Harvard Study About Preventing Panic Attacks with Good Nutrition

An article published in the Harvard Health blog by Naidoo (2019) about nutritional strategies and anxiety described that when mice were tested, researchers found that diets low in magnesium tended to increase their anxiety. Conversely, diets high in magnesium can promote calmness, which can include: leafy greens like spinach and nuts seeds, Swiss chard, whole grains, and legumes.

Here are some foods that have been shown to be very helpful in preventing anxiety:

- Foods rich in zinc have been linked to lowering anxiety: oysters, egg yolks, beef, cashews, and liver.

- A 2011 study showed that omega-3s can help reduce anxiety: fatty fish like Alaskan salmon.
- The Chinese government approved the use of asparagus extract due to its anti-anxiety properties. This approval came after a research study done by Hilmire et al. (2015; Naidoo, 2016).
- Foods rich in B vitamins like almonds and avocados have an impact on anxiety.

Good antioxidant levels are thought to help fight anxiety. A 2010 study done by Carlsen et al. revealed this information. Foods that are high in antioxidants are:

- **Beans:** Pinto, black beans, and red kidney beans
- **Fruits:** apples, black plums, prunes, and sweet cherries
- **Berries:** blackberries, blueberries, cranberries, strawberries, raspberries
- **Vegetables:** broccoli, spinach, kale, and artichokes
- **Nuts:** pecans, walnuts
- **Spices:** ginger, turmeric

With all the data showing that certain foods can help curb anxiety, it makes sense to strive for good nutrition when trying to prevent panic attacks.

Making Panic Attacks Less Intense

Is there a way to make your panic attacks less intense? As discussed, feeling like you are having a heart attack or thinking you will die are some reactions you could have to an intense panic attack. The good news is that there are things you can do for your panic attacks.

Panic attacks can come about very quickly, and it may seem like the symptoms are only going to get worse, but the truth is that, just as your panic attacks have beginnings, they also have ends. The worst thing you can do is get caught up with the intensity of your symptoms. Yes, it is natural to be overwhelmed and scared during an episode, but if you can focus on things other than your panic attack, you might have a better time.

Moreover, it may also be wise to surrender to your panic attack and just let it take its course while remembering that it won't last forever. Also, try telling yourself that the symptoms are only part of your panic attack and not a medical condition (only after your health provider has cleared you from having any medical issues)

After your panic attack, instead of obsessing about its intensity, take the time to learn more about panic attacks in general, so you can erase your fear of the unknown.

Breathing and Your Panic Attacks

A common symptom of a panic attack is shortness of breath and hyperventilation. The way to overcome this is to remember to use breathing techniques during the attack. Learn how to slow your breathing down, as taking a deep breath of air while counting to ten is a good way to combat your shortness of breath. If you need more than ten seconds, continue counting. By taking deliberate breaths, you can help yourself calm down and reduce the intensity of your panic attack.

As discussed in an earlier chapter, it is effective for you to place your hand on your stomach, so you can feel your abdomen expand when taking in a breath, and how your abdomen lowers when you expel your breath. Concentrating and focusing on something else other than the shortness of your breath can really help with that aspect of a panic attack.

Cutting Down on the Intensity of Your Panic Attack

You may feel fear and apprehension when a panic attack starts; however, you can work at not feeling overwhelmed. Changing your focus from the panic attack to something or someone else can be a great tactic for alleviating an intense panic attack.

One thing you could also do is call one of your panic attack confidants on the phone who can help you during the episode. You can also try counting to 100, or any other mental action that will distract you from your panic attack.

Manage Your Time to Relieve Stress

Break down tasks into manageable pieces and set deadlines to reach them. Don't commit to more work than you can handle. It is also good to manage your personal life in a way that gives you a structured schedule with downtime and relaxation periods. Try to set boundaries with coworkers and people in your personal life, as it is important for you to have periods of calm as often as possible.

If you are frazzled by work and your personal life, you will leave yourself open to a meltdown and possibly a severe panic attack.

What *Not* to Do

One thing that you don't want to do is have any negative self-talk, like telling yourself that you are going to die or that something terrible is going to happen to you. Try to remember positive affirmations that can replace your negative thoughts, such as "Even though I feel scared, I accept myself," "I will get through this," or "I am strong".

Self Care is Important

Even though your symptoms are extreme, there are things that you can do for yourself. It is very important that you take care of yourself, which might include lifestyle changes that can help you reduce your feelings of anxiety and stress.

As discussed before, this is the time to learn relaxation techniques, how to meditate, or try practicing yoga. Include these techniques in your daily life, so they can begin to make a difference for you.

Exercising can also help to reduce your stress and anxiety levels. Just 20 minutes every day or three times a week can be beneficial. Taking a short walk or working out in a swimming pool are also two exercise activities that can cut down on your stress.

The more you practice these activities, the more likely you will be to use these techniques when you are having a panic attack. It might be awkward to start dancing or riding away on a bicycle during an attack, but you might find that, as the symptoms lose their intensity, you might be capable of doing something unorthodox to get through your panic attacks.

Self-care is all about what makes you feel better. Don't be afraid to take up a new hobby that promotes your calmness; for example, putting together puzzles or making quilts can go a long way in supporting calmness. You can also explore spirituality as a way to bring calm into your life. These things can really help you with taking care of yourself, and they can make a difference in the way you feel every day.

While working towards vanquishing your panic attacks with self-care, you might think of keeping track of the techniques that are effective. Starting a panic diary, personal journal, or a mood and anxiety spreadsheet can be a visual reminder of what is successful for you during a panic attack, and what you need to work on in the future.

Working with Your Mental Health Providers

When working with your mental health specialist, they will design a treatment plan that is unique to you. First, they will clear you of having any other medical issues that may be causing the symptoms of your panic attack. For example, they will make sure that your heart doesn't have any issues or that you don't have asthma that might be the other reason for your shortness of breath.

As mentioned in an earlier chapter, your psychiatrist may decide to give you medication that you can take during the panic attack to calm down. Your therapist will also help you decide which strategies to use during the panic attack.

If your panic attacks are increasing, do not be afraid to tell your mental health providers. Psychiatrists and therapists will always be open to trying something different to help you. The goal is all about your wellbeing—if you believe that your mental health providers are not with you 100%, discuss your treatment concerns with them. Overall, the more you communicate with the people you have chosen to help you, the better.

Medications That Can Help

After a therapist evaluates you, they may suggest that you see a psychiatrist for medication. The following sections will break down various medications often used to treat anxiety.

Selective serotonin reuptake inhibitors (SSRIs) have a low risk of side effects; they are antidepressants and are usually the first choice your mental health provider will suggest. They are used because they help maintain a balance of serotonin in your brain. Low serotonin levels have been correlated with constant depressive feelings, so balancing serotonin can help with negative thought processes.

Serotonin and norepinephrine reuptake inhibitors (SNRIs) are another category of antidepressants that may be prescribed to you.

Designer antidepressants are another class of antidepressants that can target serotonin and neurotransmitter that can give you more energy, alertness, motivation, and attention.

Tricyclic antidepressants are an older set of antidepressants that may take longer to work than SSRIs.

Miscellaneous tranquilizers are being used because they are new and have a much lessened addictive side effect.

Benzodiazepines are a **central nervous system depressant**. It is often used as a short-term medication, as they can be addictive; however, they are effective in reducing the intensity of a panic attack. Benzodiazepines are not recommended for patients who have substance abuse issues or a history of being addicted to drugs and alcohol.

MAO inhibitors are an older type of antidepressant that allows critical neurotransmitters to remain available in the brain to regulate mood effectively. These inhibitors are rarely used because they have serious side effects, including headaches, nausea, and drowsiness.

Beta blockers are used to treat hypertension, but it has also been known to reduce anxiety. These medications help with the physical symptoms of anxiety, like shaking, trembling, rapid heartbeat, and blushing.

Atypical antipsychotics are not often prescribed for anxiety, but these medications target other neurotransmitters that SSRIs do not target, such as dopamine and noradrenaline. Prescribed at a lower dose, these medications are sometimes used in addition to SSRIs.

A psychiatrist will work with you and your therapist to find the right medications for your unique situation. In some cases, it is a hit-or-miss situation when trying to find an effective medication; therefore, it is imperative that you stay honest with your psychiatrist when searching for the right medications or combination of that will help you. Be sure to tell your psychiatrist of any medical issues or side-effects that you may be experiencing.

A complete list of medications that can be used to treat anxiety

The following is a list of the various medications that doctors may prescribe to treat anxiety. Keep in mind that you should only take these with a proper diagnosis and prescription from your doctor; make sure to work with them to figure out which medication will suit you and your situation best.

Selective serotonin reuptake inhibitors (SSRIs): Luvox (Fluvoxamine), Celexa (Citalopram), Zoloft (Sertraline), Lexapro (Escitalopram), Paxil (Paroxetine), Paxil (Paroxetine), Prozac (Fluoxetine)

Serotonin/norepinephrine reuptake inhibitors (SNRIs): Cymbalta (Duloxetine), Effexor (Venlafaxine), Pristiq (Desvenlafaxine),

Serotonin-2 antagonists reuptake inhibitors (SARIs): Desyrel (Trazodone), Serzone (Nefazodone)

Noradrenergic antidepressants (NaSSAs): Remeron (Mirtazapine)

Norepinephrine reuptake inhibitor (NRI): Wellbutrin (Bupropion)

Tricyclic antidepressants: Tofranil, Elavil, Adapin, Pamelor, Anafranil

MAO inhibitors: Nardil, Parnate, Marplan

Benzodiazepines: Ativan (lorazepam), Centrax (prazepam), Klonopin (clonazepam), Librium (chlordiazepoxide), Serax (oxazepam), Valium (diazepam), Xanax (alprazolam)

Tranquilizers that are not Benzodiazepines: Buspar (buspirone), Vistaril (hydroxyzine)

Beta Blockers: Inderal (propranolol), Tenormin (atenolol)

Atypical Antipsychotics: Risperdal (risperidone), Abilify (aripiprazole), Zyprexa (olanzapine), Seroquel (quetiapine), Geodon (ziprasidone)

Mood Stabilizers: Depakote (valproic acid), Eskalith (lithium), Lamictal (lamotrigine), Neurontin (gabapentin)

Other: Tegretol (carbamazepine), Topamax (topiramate)

Panic Attacks at Work

Unfortunately, panic attacks can't be scheduled to only happen during your personal time. There is a chance that you will have a panic attack at work. In particular, it is important that you work out a plan for what to do when you have a panic attack in this situation.

Although you may want to keep your panic attacks to yourself, it might help if you tell a supervisor or human resource staff about your panic attacks. Telling a coworker too might also be beneficial, and explaining that you have panic attacks and what you do when you have one can free up some of the stress that you have about your panic attacks happening in the workplace.

If you are having panic attacks at work, you might want to look for patterns, indicators, or triggers before the panic attack happens. If you find that there are consistent triggers in your workplace, don't quit your job just yet; remember that there are therapies like exposure therapy and CBT that can help you deal with these triggers. It *is* possible to counter the triggers that spin you into a panic attack.

Ask for Help

Discuss the difficulties you have at work with your therapist. In addition, choose a therapist who understands that you might have to contact them outside of your appointment. There are therapists who are open to receiving texts and emergency phone calls who help you through panic attacks at work.

If it isn't possible to call your therapist during this time, choose a family member, like your spouse or a sibling whom you are close to. Remember that another technique is to have an object that calms you; for example, you can choose a smooth rock or small object to keep in your pocket or purse that can make you happy and promote calmness.

Designated Safe-Spaces

You can also scout out optimal places to be when your panic attack begins. This might seem odd to you, but think about it—would you rather have a panic attack in your cubicle or outside in a peaceful place? When your panic attack starts, you can leave the office to go to your safe place. Places that you might designate as your safe place at work can be, but are not limited to: your car, a private office, a bathroom stall, or a quiet area located outside of your office.

Planning what you will do at work when a panic attack occurs is important for reducing your stress levels. You might feel mortified when thinking about the possibility of having a panic attack at the office and in front of your coworkers, but having a plan will make you feel better about being at work.

Making a Solid Plan

One thing you can take into consideration when planning is how you will leave the office and make it to your safe place. Will you tell anyone where you are going? Will you ask a coworker to come with you, so they can help? Will you stay put at your desk and do some breathing techniques to calm down enough to leave your desk and go to your safe place? Will you call your therapist or text your supervisor to let them know what is going on? Can you ask a coworker to take you home? These are some of the questions that you should think about when making a plan for when you have a panic attack at work.

Another thing to consider is writing down your plan for panic attacks at work. You can make a printable document to tape to or keep in your desk, or you can keep it digitally in your phone or on your work computer. Whatever you do, make sure that it is easy to get to when a panic attack happens (Rauch, 2016).

Overall, there are various things you can do that will help you overcome panic attacks. Don't hesitate to take care of yourself and build up your morale. Remember—panic attacks are manageable and, in some cases, completely curable.

Chapter Summary

It is possible to do things that might prevent your panic attacks, and taking care of yourself in your daily life can really make a difference. It is also important to work on techniques that will help you to avoid having a panic attack. Some of the things you can do include the following:

- Good nutrition and a good night's sleep.
- A positive outlook.
- Therapy.
- Exercise.
- Appropriate medications.
- A system for handling stress at work.

In the next chapter, you will learn about overcoming your fear of panic attacks and phobias.

CHAPTER EIGHT:

Overcoming Your Fear of Panic Attacks and Phobias

The duration of a panic attack can be as short as ten minutes, but their effects can stay with you for hours or even days after the attack. You might find that you are anxious and uneasy after an initial panic attack and the fear of having another panic attack soon after can be difficult to shake.

This uneasiness can cause you to anticipate a panic attack every hour of every day. You may begin to avoid any environments and situations that precipitate your anxiety attacks; for example, you might stop going to the mall or to the park because you had anxiety attacks in those places.

Staying away from the places that you think triggers your panic attack is not the only thing you might consider doing after an attack—you might start changing your behavior entirely because you believe that certain behaviors are causing you to have a panic attack. A common behavioral change is not going to family functions or gatherings because you have had panic attacks when surrounded by your family or in-laws.

Being Frightened and Isolating Yourself

A cycle of fear and avoidance can start once you stop going to places and start changing your behavior. Doing so creates a cycle of fear and avoidance that can negatively affect your daily functioning. It is true that you might be able to stop some of your anxiety attacks by staying home or avoiding certain people, but these tactics are usually only good for the short term.

Although panic attacks may leave you helpless, there are things you can do that don't include avoidance or isolation. You can—and as we've been doing with this book—educate yourself about panic attacks. Beyond what we've gone over so far, there may be someone in your family or friend circles who also deal with panic attacks, and there exist support groups for people who have panic attacks. These groups will help you learn about our current understanding and the practical side of panic attacks.

You can also head to the library or the internet to learn more about panic attacks. There is a lot of information out there; However, make sure you pick a reference or a website that is legitimate. You can apply the journalistic three sources rule—if you can find three references containing the same information, then there is a good chance that you are dealing with genuine fact and not mere speculation.

Accepting Panic Attacks

As we learned in chapter 4, accepting your panic attacks can help with the intensity of the panic attack. It's a hard reality to live with, but you can make peace with knowing that you are prone to these kinds of episodes. Just remember that you have the power to do something about them and that it is important to reach out and get help.

When possible, change your response to your panic attacks and do something positive after an attack that empowers you. Vow to learn routines and behaviors that will support you and make you stronger. Become an observer of your panic attack and not a victim when it happens, and do the same positive things after each panic attack. Don't let the panic attack win—stand firm and resolve to conquer your panic attacks. Keep practicing the techniques you are learning in therapy, your support group, or from this book.

Furthermore, it is important that you prepare for when you have a panic attack. For example, always have your panic attack journal at the ready, so you can jot down what is happening before, during, and after an attack. Try rehearsing what you are going to ask of the people you have chosen to help you during a panic attack, and become familiar with the things you are going to do during an episode, so when it happens, you can do what you need to do during the attack.

How to Deal with Specific Phobias

Sometimes, the root of the problem with panic attacks is that you have a specific phobia of a person, place, or thing. Perhaps something traumatic happened to you, and you developed a phobia after the fact. Phobias can be a major trigger for panic attacks.

For example, if you were attacked by a rabid dog and survived, you might always be scared of any dog that crosses your path. You may, in fact, go out of your way to completely avoid any dogs in general, including changing your walking route, avoiding a friend's house if they own a dog, and never owning a dog yourself.

Specific phobias have the best prognosis of any anxiety disorder. If you work hard in therapy, you may be able to cure any anxiety you have toward your phobia. There is strong evidence that CBT can cure the anxiety attacks that are linked to phobias.

One of the main tenets of cognitive behavioral therapy is desensitizing you to the object that you fear; sticking with the earlier example about fear of dogs, your therapist might take you to an animal shelter to be around dogs that are locked in their kennels. The belief is that once you are desensitized towards your phobia, the panic attacks will cease.

Although it is not exactly certain why people have panic attacks, mental health professionals have suggested that the main cause of panic attacks are certain phobias. The good news is that if a phobia is the reason for your panic attack, you have a good prognosis for treating your panic attack.

Cognitive Behavioral Therapy

Cognitive behavioral therapy, or **CBT**, has been found to be effective at curing phobias. Perhaps there is a certain behavior that you have to work through or negative self-talk that reinforces the fear you have toward your object of anxiety. CBT will help you sort out these actions.

One practice, which is an extension of CBT, is **exposure therapy**, and it is a technique that is especially effective in treating anxiety attacks. Exposure therapy is a behavioral therapy that helps people with problematic fears. When a therapist uses exposure therapy to treat panic disorder, they systematically expose the patient to the events or environments that trigger their panic attacks. The therapist would create a safe environment for you to experience stressful situations.

Exposure Therapy

Exposure therapy is appropriate for people who have panic attacks due to a traumatic memory or a phobia. If you avoid these situations, you will probably isolate yourself unhealthily, which isn't good. The fear and avoiding isolation can amplify your fears, making it hard for you to lead a regular and stress-free life. For example, if you have a fear of bumblebees, you may go from simply avoiding places with beehives to not going outside at all.

Developed in the early 1900s, exposure therapy was used by behaviorists like Ivan Pavlov and John Watson. Pavlov is most famous for his classical conditioning of dogs, during an experiment in which he trained dogs to salivate when he rang a bell.

Behaviorist Joseph Wolpe developed a systematic desensitization technique in 1958, where he used relaxation training, anxiety hierarchy, and exposure to lessen a patient's sensitivity to situations that the patient dreaded or was afraid of. In the 1970s, more was done to develop exposure therapy.

The types of exposure therapy are as follows:

Imaginal Exposure: A patient is asked to deal with their fears by picturing the situation in their mind. By picturing a crowded mall, a person with the fear of being in crowds can systematically work through their anxiety.

In Vivo Exposure: A patient is exposed to real-life situations that would cause them fear and stress. For example, a patient who has a fear of dogs might go to the nearest rescue shelter and view the dogs while they are in their pens.

Virtual Reality Exposure: This is where virtual reality is used to treat a patient's fear. The situation is fabricated to feel like the real thing; for example, a person afraid of heights may experience a virtual reality simulation of climbing down a tall building.

Aside from these forms of exposure therapy, there are other, more specific exposure therapy techniques:

Systematic Desensitization: This technique implements relaxation training and the development of an anxiety hierarchy, in which you rank your fears or phobias on a simple scale of 1-10. Learned relaxation techniques offset stress and anxiety.

Graded Exposure: This technique uses the concept of desensitization to help quell a patient's anxiety.

Flooding: A patient is exposed in vivo or imaginal to his anxiety-evoking events for a prolonged time. This therapy is done until the anxiety is diminished significantly (Exposure Therapy, 2015).

Prolonged Exposure (PE): This is similar to flooding, but psychoeducation and cognitive processing are used. This is an effective treatment for trauma-related issues.

Exposure and Response Prevention (ERP): This form of therapy decreases the link between compulsions and obsessions. A therapist will provoke an obsession in the patient, then ask them not to engage themselves in their compulsions or behavioral rituals. This option is good for patients who are working to rid themselves of any obsessions and compulsions.

Exposure Therapy and Its Successes

A clinician who treats patients with exposure therapy regards anxiety as a false alarm to a person, place, or thing. This anxiety is overblown and not appropriate to the feared object, and the proportion of the patient's fear is not in line with the reaction of others.

The more a patient removes or avoids the object of fear from their vicinity, the less chance they will have to discover the inappropriateness of his response to anxiety. A person might understand in their mind that being afraid of their object of fear is ridiculous or overblown, but deep in their mind, they would still harbor an intense fear. In kind, this intense fear quite often leads to panic attacks.

An example of how a therapist may manage treatment during exposure therapy is as follows:

1. Provides ongoing assessments of the patient's fears.
2. There is a tailored education about the anxiety that the patient is experiencing.
3. Provides strategies, such as mindfulness, and encourages the patient to practice these strategies when dealing with their phobia(s).
4. Graded exposure to the object of fear.
5. A program of cognitive interventions that will identify and challenge faulty or negative thinking.

Cognitive restructuring and medication are also used as supplemental techniques for helping patients undergoing exposure therapy.

The following section outlines an example of graded therapy. In this case, the patient is afraid of lizards.

1. The patient will be required to look at pictures of lizards.
2. The patient will then be required to touch the picture of lizards.
3. Next, they will be told to look at live lizards on the internet.
4. The patient will then touch a fake lizard.

5. The patient will touch the glass or top of a container that is displaying live lizards.
6. The patient will then imagine what it is like to touch a lizard.
7. Finally, the patient will touch a live lizard.

Exposure therapy can be very difficult for a person with panic attacks; however, it is important to stick with the therapy as long as possible for it to take effect. Research has shown that exposure therapy can be very effective, so it is important to participate as well as possible when in this form of therapy.

Chapter Summary

Fear and phobias are major components of panic attacks. The sooner you deal with them, the better your ability to prevent future panic attacks. It is possible to overcome your fears about panic attacks by educating yourself, changing your responses, and practicing acceptance of your panic attacks.

Exposure therapy helps to desensitize you to your phobias. You will go through several steps to reach a point where you are not at the mercy of your phobias, including:

- Looking at pictures of your phobia.
- Touching pictures of your phobia.
- Looking at your phobia "live."
- Touching a fake item of your phobia.
- Touching your phobia through a glass case.
- Imagining how it would feel to touch your phobia.
- Actually touching your phobia.

CHAPTER NINE:

Cognitive Behavioral Therapy and EMDR Therapy: Treatment without Medication

When you are ready to start healing yourself, it is time to look into some therapeutic options. Indeed, science may fully understand what causes panic attacks, but that does not mean that specific types of helpful therapy don't exist.

Some of these therapies include:

- Panic-focused psychodynamic psychotherapy (PFPP)
- Cognitive behavioral therapy (CBT)
- Eye Movement Desensitization and Reprocessing (EMDR)

The course of therapy that we will describe in chapter 9 is cognitive behavioral therapy (CBT), which is a form of therapy that has proven to be effective in treating panic attacks. It is known to be goal-oriented with quick results, as you will likely see. The success of CBT and quick results is a reason that therapists prefer it to treat patients suffering from panic attacks.

Cognitive Behavioral Therapy

Cognitive behavioral therapy (CBT) is psychotherapy used by therapists who treat various psychological disorders, ranging from anxiety to bipolar disorder. CBT is a psychotherapy that focuses on a person's thoughts, feelings, perceptions, and how they act upon those feelings. Therapists who use CBT believe that your thoughts, perceptions, and feelings influence your behavior (Star, 2019).

A tenet of CBT is that you might not be able to change what is going on in your life, but you *can* change the way you perceive your life.

When you see a therapist for your panic attacks with CBT, they will help you become more aware of your conscious thoughts. For example, a therapist will weed out the negative or faulty thought processes that have appeared and become bad habits in your daily life.

CBT has proven to be effective in patients who suffer from a major depressive disorder, post-traumatic stress disorder (PTSD), addiction, and general phobias. CBT has proven very successful, and many therapists have also used it to treat patients with irritable bowel syndrome (IBS), chronic fatigue (Star), and fibromyalgia.

Mainly, CBT offers you the chance to exchange your negative thoughts and actions into more positive thoughts and actions.

Dealing with Negative Thoughts

When you have a panic attack, you are dealing with self-deprecating beliefs and negative thoughts. It can also happen that, in your daily life, you have many negative thoughts. Being afraid and having negative thinking can all link back to panic attacks. The primary goal of CBT is to help patients overcome negative thinking and replace it with positive thoughts and healthier actions.

There are not only mental components to panic attacks, but physical components as well. The somatic symptoms of a panic attack may include chest pains, shortness of breath, rapid heartbeat, and heavy sweating. These symptoms can all overwhelm a person who is having a panic attack; therefore, a person who regularly suffers from panic attacks may develop distressing thoughts and fears of going crazy, dying, and/or losing control (Star, 2019).

The result of a panic attack is that a person may become terrified of the triggers that appeared before their panic attack. For example, if you generally have a panic attack when you go to the dentist, merely being within the dentist's office waiting room before they work on your teeth would probably cause you to go into a panic attack. From that moment on, you would have a remarkable fear of going to the dentist's office, so you would cease to go all together, even if you develop a major toothache and your gums swell. In this case, the disruption to your life is that you would rather go through immense physical pain than go to visit a professional specially trained to alleviate your tooth and gums pain.

The longer you avoid the dentist's office, the more scared you would become, which is a typical result for anyone who stays away from the things they fear.

When you begin CBT, you might not be able to control when you have a panic attack, but you can learn some brilliant coping mechanisms that could help you to deal with your panic attacks.

The Processes of CBT

There are certain processes that you will go through when you participate in cognitive behavioral therapy. According to Star (2019), they are the following:

1. Notice and take charge of your negative thoughts—first, you will identify your negative cognitions or thinking patterns.
2. Participate in activities and exercises that will help you notice your negative thoughts much easier. When you are involved in these activities, you will learn healthier thought processes, and you might even have homework that could help you identify your faulty thinking.
3. You will be asked to do writing exercises. By writing down your thinking, you can evaluate and recognize your faulty thinking. Once you have isolated this kind of thinking, you can replace it with healthier thinking that does not bring you down or trigger your panic attacks. For these exercises, you can make a journal specific to what you are writing; for example, different journals for your thoughts and feelings, some affirmations you have come up with, what you feel gratitude for, or a journal for documenting and describing your panic attacks.
4. You will be working on behavioral changes and skill-building. In this stage, you will learn how to reconfigure your maladaptive behaviors while building and using healthy coping strategies (Star, 2019). At this stage, you will focus on learning skills that can help you manage your stress and anxiety, along with skills to help you make it through your panic attacks. You will probably be told to rehearse these new skills in therapy and be encouraged to practice them daily, beyond therapy.

5. Desensitization is a frequently used CBT technique that will help you to gradually learn to cope with anxiety-producing stimuli. Furthermore, you will learn to manage any anxious feelings you may have. Your therapist will slowly introduce you to more anxiety-inducing affairs, and you will continue to work through your feelings of panic and fear.

6. Learning to remain calm during a panic attack will be taught to you in therapy. CBT helps you reduce the symptoms of your particular panic attacks. There may sometimes be other treatment options, like medication, that your therapist will recommend along with working through CBT. The main goal for your therapist is to help develop a plan for treatment that is best for you.

EMDR Therapy

An effective treatment for panic attacks is **Eye Movement Desensitization and Reprocessing (EMDR)**. According to Gotter (2019), this therapy is an interactive psychotherapy technique used to relieve psychological stress.

EMDR is a therapy that helps you become less emotionally upset by diverting your attention. When your attention is diverted, you will be more likely to be less emotional. The whole point of this therapy is to diminish the impact that these emotionally upsetting memories may carry. EMDR is a good therapy for those patients who may find it difficult to talk about their traumatic past.

EMDR is used to treat the following disorders:

- Depression.
- Anxiety.
- Panic attacks and panic disorder.

- Eating disorders.
- Addiction.

How Does EMDR Help Patients?

Patients being treated with EMDR have to commit to at least 12 separate therapy sessions, which is broken down into eight phases. These phases are the following:

Phase 1: History and treatment planning

This is the phase in which your therapist learns more about the trauma and painful memories that you are dealing with. In this session, you may also want to talk about the things you know trigger your panic attacks or suspected triggers. Your therapist will then decide what treatment you should receive.

Phase 2: Preparation

During this phase, your therapist will work with you to decide on strategies you can use before or during your panic attacks. Your therapist will most likely teach you stress management techniques, like mindfulness and deep breathing in this stage.

Phase 3: Assessment

During this phase, your therapist will decide on specific memories that they will be working on with you, along with all the components associated with those memories. Specifically, they will be trying to deduce the physical sensations that you feel when you focus on an event.

Phases 4-7: Treatment

Gotter (2019) explains that this phase of the treatment is when your therapist will actually begin with your treatment. During your session, you will be asked to focus on a negative image, thought, or memory.

While you are doing this, your therapist will simultaneously ask you to do specific eye movements. Gotter says that "the bilateral stimulation may also include taps or other movements mix in, depending on your case."

After you do bilateral stimulation, you will be asked to make your mind blank and recall your thoughts and feelings. When you recall these thoughts, your therapist might ask you to refocus on the memory or have you start thinking about another traumatic memory.

If the traumatic memory is too much for you, your therapist will bring you back into the present before they would have you recall another traumatic memory. While working through the phases of EMDR, the upsetting thoughts and feelings associated with your traumatic memory should also start to fade.

Phase 8: Evaluation

In this phase, you and your therapist will be talking about the progress you are making in EMDR therapy. For example, are the traumatic memories still painful, or have the feelings associated with that memory begun to fade?

Various studies done on the effects of EMDR have displayed the practice as positive with significant changes in their patients. In this case, EMDR would be another option for you when seeking treatment for your panic attacks.

Chapter Summary

It is possible to receive treatment for your panic attacks that doesn't include medication. CBT and EMDR are two of the most common therapies to treat panic attacks. The CBT process includes:

- Recognizing and replacing negative thoughts.
- Writing exercises.
- Skill building and behavioral changes.
- Desensitization.
- Relaxation techniques.

In the next chapter, you will learn more about getting help for panic attacks.

CHAPTER TEN:

Getting Help for Panic Attacks

Panic attacks can be quite overwhelming, and having random attacks can disrupt your life. Consequently, it is imperative that you do something to help your attacks to either go away or become less intense.

So far in this book, we have discussed strategies such as exposure therapy and cognitive behavioral therapy that are both excellent in helping you cease or lessen your panic attacks. In this chapter, we will be looking at some more therapeutic options that you can do to decrease the intensity of your panic attacks or end them altogether.

Therapy requires a lot of commitment and hard work, but if done correctly, the results can be very effective. The key is to find the right kind of therapy for your unique needs.

Cognitive Behavior Modification

Sometimes we find ourselves engaging in a lot of negative self-talk. Clinicians believe that negative self- talk may contribute to or be the catalyst for your panic attacks. Psychologist Donald Meichenbaum developed **cognitive behavior modification**, or

CBM, to focus on identifying dysfunctional self-talk. When you identify behaviors and patterns that may hinder your recovery, you can make significant progress to leading a better life. Meichenbaum believed that behaviors have outcomes that manifest themselves due to our own self-verbalizations. This is why it is so important to have positive thoughts. When you reduce your negative self-talk and change to positive thoughts, you may see an improvement or complete cessation of your panic attacks.

Rational Emotive Behavior Therapy

Albert Ellis developed **rational emotive behavior (REBT).** REBT is a cognitive behavior technique known to be effective in the treatment of panic disorders (Ankrom, 2019). Ellis, thus, developed a therapy that helps patients to identify and dispute negative thoughts or "irrational beliefs." For example, telling yourself constantly that you don't measure up to regular people can be a thought that causes deep psychological problems. By identifying that this statement or thought is not true, and why it isn't true, you can begin to reduce the frequency and intensity of your panic attacks.

Being in therapy and using the REBT technique can work to change your brain, so you cope better with your panic attacks or cease having them altogether.

Panic-focused Psychodynamic Therapy

Panic-focused psychodynamic therapy (PFPP) is a type of panic disorder therapy based on specific psychoanalytic concepts. This therapy emphasizes the theory that people are defined by early human experiences, and that unconscious motives and psychological conflicts are at the core of your current behavior (Ankrom, 2019).

PFPP therapists make the assumption that the unconscious mind hides painful emotions and defense mechanisms that may be keeping our painful emotions hidden; therefore, PFPP therapy helps bring emotions that we have hidden in our subconscious into the forefront of our mind, so we can better deal with these emotions. When this is done, your panic disorder symptoms can either be alleviated or eliminated.

Group Therapy

Sometimes, going about it alone in therapy can be too much. If this is the case, perhaps group therapy would work better for you. **Group therapy** is often made up of people who are experiencing the same or similar problems that you are having. It is based on the principle that you can learn from one another about techniques that will help you to diminish or stop your panic attacks.

Some benefits of group therapy include:

- A minimization of the shame and stigma by sharing experiences with other people who have similar symptoms and challenges.
- Other group members can provide you with inspiration and reinforcement by modeling the healthy actions that you are learning in group therapy.
- Group therapy can naturally provide an "exposure environment" for you to learn how to diminish your fear of having panic symptoms in social situations.

Overall, you should feel completely safe when attending a group therapy session. The group that you join can have anywhere between 2-10 or more people in attendance. There is often a therapist or counselor that leads the group. In some instances, the group is run by an experienced person, and topics are brought up and discussed by the group. The therapist or group leader will encourage you and the others to talk about your panic attacks and ultimately your fears in a safe space.

Couples and Family Therapy

Even though having a panic attack is a singular experience, you are not alone—friends and family members are also affected by your panic attacks, and the people who love you will be concerned about the intense symptoms of your panic attacks. It is hard to see someone you love going through something as overwhelming as panic episodes.

Some patients have found that going to **couples** or **family therapy** can address issues that had begun forming in the minds of their family members, significant others, and/or friends. Family therapy addresses topics such as your dependency needs caused by your panic attacks; questions and concerns that your family and friends have about giving you support; and general communication and education about your panic attacks.

Couples and family therapy can help to improve your environment. Moreover, therapy can help you with eliminating certain cues or triggers that might be caused by the discord that exists in your family or friend circle. However, it may be necessary for you to also go to individual therapy as well as couples or family therapy in order to work out the issues that cause your panic attacks. In particular, it is important for you to pick a therapy that addresses your unique needs.

Reasons to Participate in Therapy

Panic attacks affect about 6 million adults in the United States, which counts for 2.7% of the population. Panic attacks are more likely to occur in women than in men according to the Anxiety and Depression Association of America (n.d.).

It might be hard to go to a therapist for help with your panic attacks. You may believe that your panic attacks are untreatable, but this isn't true. Many people find relief from their panic attacks when they start attending therapy. It is true that going to therapy and doing all the things that your therapist asks of you can be very hard, but the alternative is to endure infinite and random panic attacks that are so intense that they regularly interfere with your daily life.

The following list brings to light various reasons why people avoid getting help for their panic attacks ("Panic and Panic Disorder," 2019):

- They are more prone to alcohol or drug abuse.
- They have already become financially dependent on others.
- They have experienced a decline in health.
- They have attempted suicide.
- They have become homebound due to the development of **agoraphobia** (fear of going outside and avoidance of things that may cause panic or anxiety in the individual).

Another important reason for going to therapy is that a therapist can help reassure you that you are not "going crazy."

Ten Ways to Find a Good Therapist

The most important thing to do when deciding to ask for help is to find a good therapist, but how do you find a good therapist? Here are five strategies you can use to find a good therapist.

1. Ask your family doctor if they work with any psychiatrists or therapists. Furthermore, you can ask them who they would go to if they were having severe panic attacks. Your family doctor works with other health care professionals, so they would be a good person to ask.

2. Friends and family may surprise you with how much they know about mental health; in fact, you may find that some of your friends or family are in therapy or have friends who go to therapy. Consequently, they may be able to give you contact information for a therapist who would work well for you.

3. Ask if your place of employment has an Employee Assistance Program (EAP), and the place to find out would be your human resource department. EAP services may be provided at work or be outsourced. Counseling might also be an employee benefit that you could take advantage of.

4. Your insurance company will most likely have a list of psychiatrists and therapists who are covered by your insurance. If you need help selecting a therapist from their list, ask to be assigned to a caseworker or nurse provided by your insurance for help.

5. A search for "therapist" and "panic attacks" on the internet may also be an effective strategy for finding a good mental health professional. Many mental health professionals have websites or blogs that can also help you get to know them better. Listings on the internet often have the areas of treatment that they offer, so

choose a professional who has experience with panic attacks and has good therapy results for your case.

In the past, if you lived in a small or rural town, it was almost impossible to find a mental health practitioner; however, many therapists are now also on Skype, Facetime, or have a general telephone. This is good if you live in a small town with limited resources, or if you are too busy to travel to a therapist's office. In fact, sometimes a combination of phone therapy and face-to-face contact is good for helping with social phobias that you have developed due to panic attacks.

While doing your search, get at least three references from each source that you can ask. The more mental health professionals you contact, the better your chances of finding a therapist or doctor who will be the perfect fit.

Questions for Your Therapist

Going to a therapist may be a new experience for you. You may have doubts and anxiety about working with a therapist and discussing your panic attacks. Specifically, it is important to go prepared for your first appointments. Here are some questions that you might want to ask or discuss with a mental health professional:

- What can I do about the intensity of my symptoms? Can you help me with some relaxation techniques?
- My symptoms are very intense. What is going on in my brain and body that causes such strong symptoms?
- Is it possible to learn how to stop a panic attack?
- Could there be any physical conditions that are causing my panic attacks?
- Is there anything I should avoid, like certain foods, beverages, or medications?

- I would like to explore factors in my environment or personal relationships that could be triggering my panic attacks. Can you help me with this?
- Do you work with any psychiatrists that could help me with my medication needs? Can you refer me to someone whom you trust?
- What kinds of therapies do you offer? Specifically, are you familiar with any forms of therapy that have been successful in ceasing or alleviating panic attacks?
- What types of therapy would you suggest for me?

These are all great starting points and questions for when you are interviewing a therapist and deciding who might be a good fit for you. You can decide which questions fit your situation best and go from there.

Going to a Psychiatrist.

After a therapist evaluates you, they may suggest that you see a psychiatrist for medication. Some medications used to manage the symptoms of panic attacks have been discussed in chapter 7.

A psychiatrist will examine you and work with your therapist to find the right medications for your unique situation. Be sure to tell your psychiatrist of any medical issues or side effects that you are prone to experience, and if you have any allergies to a specific medication.

Although you might be overwhelmed by your panic attacks, it is important that you ask for help. There are many different forms of therapy that can successfully treat your panic disorder. There also exist various medications that can help with your therapy as well.

We may not know exactly what causes a panic attack, but there are proven methods that can help you deal with the intensity of your panic attacks and, ultimately, along the many avenues of help that are available, you can finally eradicate your panic attacks once and for all.

Chapter Summary

In this chapter, you learned that there are six common types of therapy to treat panic attacks. These types are: CBT, CBM, REBT, panic-focused psychodynamic therapy, group therapy, and couples and family therapy.

There are also several different ways for you to find a therapist. These methods include the following:

- Asking your PCP doctor for a referral.
- Asking friends and family about any therapists they know.
- Going through your insurance company.

FINAL WORDS

If you've ever experienced a panic attack, you know that having an attack can feel like your world has just blown up. Your body has symptoms that are so severe, you may think that you are dying. It is one thing to have a single panic attack, but to have several at rando—well, this can make life quite hard to lead. Having a panic attack with no intervention can scare you so much that you drop out of activities and live in fear that you will have another attack; in fact, there are two known conditions when it comes to panic attacks: anticipatory anxiety and phobic avoidance. These two symptoms of a panic attack can take you out of the game quite literally. Leaving the house because you fear there will be a trigger is very real to a person who suffers from these types of attacks.

Although panic attacks can be overwhelming and intense, there is a way out. There are many forms of therapies and strategies that can help you if you suffer from episodes. The techniques in this book, if done diligently, can go a long way toward making your panic attacks less intense and, in some cases, stop altogether. In this book, we explored the definition of a panic attack, myths and misconceptions, how to stop panic attacks, powerful relaxation techniques, ways to prevent panic attacks, and how to get help.

The central theme of this book has been to give the message that panic attacks can be stopped. It takes hard work in therapy and on your own, but there are ways to stop your attacks.

It is important to believe that you can conquer your panic attacks. In this book, we myth-busted misconceptions about panic attacks, and you discovered that you can't die from a panic attack and that panic attacks won't make you insane.

Panic attacks are not a joke—they may come at you big and take no prisoners. However, you can always follow the techniques outlined in this book to make the fight fair; for example, being calm and accepting the panic attack is one place to start. You may believe that the only way through a panic attack is to "panic" and become agitated, but it doesn't have to be this way. You can be firm and follow the five steps of AWARE: acknowledge and accept; wait and watch (or work); actions (that make you more comfortable); repeat the above steps; and finally, end. If you learn to do these five steps, you will be well on your way to making it through your panic attacks.

The hardest part about panic attacks is that there is no known hard and fast cause for them. It gets confusing because if we don't know what causes a panic attack, how can we treat them? How can we make them stop happening? Despite not knowing the cause of panic attacks, mental health providers have developed successful ways for treating them. I discussed these strategies in this book and stand behind them.

When you manage to do the five steps of AWARE, don't stop there. Get out in front of the panic attack and do the steps you learned in chapter 5. Know your triggers and limit your stimuli to prevent a panic attack from happening. When you start to panic, relax and do some deep breathing or relax your muscles, one group at a time, so you can release the tension that has developed across your body. Visualize your happy place and be strict about your negative thoughts—work on not having them. Completely kick them out of your mind and, above all, practice mindfulness and live in the present—not the future or the past. These techniques work because they address your stress responses, including any increased heart rate, tense muscles, and rapid breathing.

Relaxing and taking care of the stressors in your life is also important. It is not enough to know your triggers because you must also make sure you are not overwhelmed or stressed out. You have to be proactive and eat the right foods, get enough sleep, and manage your time, so you don't become overburdened.

The most important thing you can do if you are having a panic attack is to reach out for help. Your first step was reading this book, and your next step will be to do the strategies we have discussed. Beyond that, you might want to find a therapist or let your friends and family know how they can help you. Have a plan for when you have a panic attack and assign a person who will be with you at work or home to help you when you are having an episode. Reaching out to a therapist is also important. With the six common types of therapies, you can rest assured that you will be able to find a treatment that will be effective for you.

Don't be afraid of sharing with others the difficulty that you are having due to your panic attacks. Couple and family therapy can really help connect with the people who care about you. Although you may feel alone when you are suffering from panic attacks, remember that you are not. The people in your life are going through these attacks with you, and it is the most natural thing in the world for them to want to support and help you. Don't be afraid to reach out and include them in your treatment plans.

My greatest wish is that this book will help or has helped you find your way out of having panic attacks. Good luck, and don't lose faith!

APPENDIX

For your convenience, I have gathered together the 23 relaxation techniques mentioned in the book.

The first of the five steps of AWARE is to acknowledge and accept what is happening during a panic attack. It is even possible to stop the panic attack with the five steps of AWARE. The first thing that you must do is acknowledge and accept your anxiety ("How to Stop Panic Attacks," n.d.) The first of the five steps of AWARE is to acknowledge and accept what is happening during a panic attack. It is even possible to stop the panic attack with the five steps of AWARE. The first thing that you must do is acknowledge and accept your anxiety ("How to Stop Panic Attacks, n.d.)

The next step of AWARE is *wait*. When you have a panic attack, you probably experience the need to flee or struggle; however, rash action will only make things worse. Often, when you have a panic attack, you are reduced to a state in which you cannot think straight; therefore, you are more prone to do something rash. Moreover, you make decisions that may just make your circumstances worse.

The next thing you want to do is *watch*. This is the time to try to understand how your panic attack works. What was happening before you had the attack and what is happening during the attack are both important aspects to observe. By observing these actions, you have the opportunity to start a panic diary that can help you notice important parts of the panic attack.

You can also add "work" to this step. When you are having a panic attack, you might not be able to wait and watch immediately—this is where "work" comes in. For example, say you are driving your car or giving a presentation. Don't freak out and run from this event, but instead, remain engaged in what you are doing and calmly move toward watching and waiting while you are having your panic attack.

So, what do you do when a panic attack happens? Well, your job is to make yourself more comfortable with the attack. Some techniques that have been helpful to people who have panic attacks include:

- Belly breathing or diaphragmatic breathing.
- Talking yourself through the attack.
- Getting involved with your present.
- Working with your body.

When you find yourself entering a new cycle of an intense panic attack, keep your wits about you and start the AWARE cycle all over again. It might be hard for you to do, but if you acknowledge and accept that you are having a longer panic attack, you will be able to wait and watch (and possibly continue on with the work aspect). Then, you can get into *action* and make yourself more comfortable until the panic attack eventually ends.

The final step of aware is to *end* the panic attack.

Although you might think it is impossible to do anything during a panic attack but feel terror, it is possible to do something to quell the attack. The best thing to do is teach yourself to focus and do things that will break your concentration away from the attack.

1. Teach yourself to focus

It is very important that you don't fight the panic attack or get over-excited. If you are calm and accept that you are having an attack, there is a chance that the symptoms of the attack will not be as intense as they could be.

2. Asking for help

It may be helpful to talk to your doctor about finding a good psychiatrist or therapist, as they may be able to refer you to mental health professionals that they have a working relationship with. In this way, you will have a team that can work out a care plan that is unique and effective to you.

3. Controlling your breath

Deep breathing and counting slowly to four while you are breathing in and out can be a great help. If you continue to breathe rapidly, it may increase your anxiety and cause extreme tension in your body, resulting in other physical symptoms like a tight or heavy feeling in your chest. Therefore, it is important to concentrate on controlling your breathing.

If you breathe deeply, like you are filling up a balloon, your breath can help fill your lungs slowly and steadily (Crawford, 2018). Counting slowly as you expand your lungs or abdomen can help you concentrate on something else besides your panic attack, and this concentration can consequently help you to get through your panic attack.

4. Medications for your panic attack

There are various other techniques that can help you during an attack, but something to consider is taking medications to help quell your episodes. If you're treated by a psychiatrist or your primary caregiver, you may be prescribed medication to help you get through the intensity of a panic attack. This medication may be prescribed to take regularly in the morning, night, or during the day. Moreover, you may be given medicines to take PRN, which means that you would take this medication when you need it.

5. Avoid bombarding your senses

If you have panic attacks due to overwhelming stimuli, it is important that you learn to stay away from bright light and sounds when possible. If you can't prevent your exposure and find that bright lights are triggering your panic attack, try to remove yourself from the central area of the lights. If that isn't an option, find a spot in the room where your exposure is limited and try to focus on your breathing or any other action that you believe can help lessen the intensity of your panic attack.

6. Panic attacks and triggers

How do you become aware of the triggers that may be causing your panic attacks? One thing you can do is keep a journal or a diary about the events that trigger your panic attacks.

By keeping a diary about your panic attacks, you might notice patterns or indications that certain situations are causing your panic attacks. Until you can work through these situations with your therapist, it is wise to be aware of the things that may be triggering you; however, do not go to the extreme of staying at home or not participating in something that is healthy for you just because your participation may expose you to something that triggers you. In therapy, you can work toward desensitizing yourself to situations that come before you have a panic attack. It is important that you learn your triggers and work actively toward dealing with them healthily.

7. Exercising to release endorphins

Another healthy way to deal with a panic attack is light exercise. Even though there really is no way to prepare for a panic attack, exercising is something that can still make you feel better.

Exercise is more than just toning your body and burning calories—it helps release endorphins in your body that can improve your mood and relax your body (Crawford, 2018).

When you do something as simple as walking, you release the endorphins into your system. Even walking can help you deal with a stressful environment. A short walk during a stressful time can help you regulate your breathing and release any nervous tension that has built up in you when stressed.

Walking during a panic attack can help you focus on something other than what is causing the panic. It can also help with the powerful feelings of fight or flight. In sum, there are many benefits of light exercise when you are having to cope with panic attacks.

8. Being mindful

Mindfulness is the state of being conscious of what is happening around you. Being mindful can aid you in dealing with the present—not the past or future. It is great to use for achieving awareness of the present moment, accepting that you are having a panic attack, and becoming aware of your bodily sensations, thoughts, and feelings.

A therapist might tell you that mindfulness is paying attention on purpose (Niemiec, 2017). Sometimes, when you have a panic attack, you might get the feeling that you are detached from reality; however, there are exercises you can do while having a panic attack that can bring you back to yourself. Some examples of these exercises are the following:

- Listen for four distinct sounds and think of why they are all different from each other.
- Pull your attention to five different things around you and consider why each one is different from the other.
- Choose three objects and describe to yourself how they are different. Reasons can include different textures, uses, and temperatures.
- Focus on one or two different smells around you. What are they and have you smelled them before?
- Taste something: a candy that you carry in your pocket or purse, for example.

Doing exercises such as these will pull your focus away from the panic attack and bring you back to the present (Legg, 2018).

9. Focusing on one object

Being mindful is a good way to stay in the present and focus; however, it might be hard at first to be mindful without a bit of practice. One thing you can do to become good at being mindful is to master the art of focusing on one object.

This simple task can really help you while you are having a panic attack. Just pick one object near you and focus on it completely. Study that object and determine its qualities to help you focus. What color is the shape? What texture is it? Questions like this can help you tune into that focus.

10. Muscle relaxation

The key to this exercise is to slow down your breathing and give yourself permission to relax. When you are calm, your breathing slows down and you can concentrate on your muscle groups and tell yourself mentally to relax. This exercise, or PMR, is simply focusing on each set of muscles in your body and visualizing the muscles relaxing.

There are many different muscle groups that you can focus on; there is a lot to remember, but you can start with your arms, then your head, neck, shoulders, chest, hips, then, lastly, your legs and your feet. One by one, you would tense these muscle groups, feel the tension for 5 seconds, then release these muscles and relax for ten seconds. Do this with your whole body. This has a two-fold purpose—first, it gives you something to focus on; and second, you would relax the muscles that have become very tense during your panic attack.

11. Find your happy place

In everyone's experience, there is a place where we are happy and at our best. Perhaps it is a bench in a beautiful park or somewhere at the beach. Each person has their very own happy place.

If it is hard for you to focus on something in the room, close your eyes and bring into your vision the place where you are most happy. Take a moment to think about how you feel when you are in this happy place—consider as many details as you can and completely focus on your place of choice.

When you are having a panic attack, it is important for you to slow down time as much as possible. When you are thinking of your happy place, think of details that require you to focus. Remembering how a place smells, sounds, and feels, as this is a simple way of getting yourself to focus. You don't necessarily have to remember details, like how many stairs up there are from the beach to the patio or the exact color of the walls in your happy place. Just keep it simple.

When you've thought of the details of your happy place, concentrate on being there in your mind. Take slow breaths through your nose and mouth, and focus on your breathing and the details of your place of choice. Continue to do this until the panic attack starts to go away (Legg, 2018).

12. Finding a mantra

A mantra is a word, phrase, or sound that can help you focus (Crawford, 2018). For example, I like to think of the word "happy" when I am stressed. You may have a word or phrase that makes you happy, such as "there's no place like home."

By chanting this mantra, you are taking your mind off the panic attack and toward something positive for yourself. Another good phrase to use during a panic attack is "This too shall pass." This specific mantra not only takes your focus off your panic attack, but it also gives you confidence that what you are going through will end, and that it can't last forever.

When you find your mantra, try it and see how it helps you regulate your breathing and relax your muscles. This is a good step to alleviating your panic attacks, as it not only helps you relax, but a good mantra can also soothe and help you take the anxiety away.

13. Finding help during your panic attacks

When you are experiencing a panic attack, it is good to have some help. Perhaps you have a spouse or a friend whom you can tell about your panic attacks. Pick an important person in your life to help you with the panic attack when it happens.

This person could act like a coach who helps you get through a tough spot by reminding you to do the techniques that best help you when you are having a panic attack.

14. Breathing techniques

- Ask someone to find you a quiet and comfortable place for you to sit while you are experiencing your panic attack.
- When you are seated in a quiet spot, put one hand on your stomach and the other on your chest, then breathe deeply. You can inhale and imagine your abdomen filling up with air like a balloon.
- Take a slow and regular breath in through your nose. Watch and sense your hands as you breathe in. The hand on your chest should remain still, while the hand on your stomach would move slightly.
- Breathe out through your mouth slowly.
- Repeat this process at least ten times, or until you begin to feel your anxiety quiet down.

Another breathing technique you can use is to let your thumb and middle finger pinch your nostrils shut. Lift your middle finger and breath in while watching the hand on your stomach move. Hold your breath and let your middle finger close your nostril once again. Next, it's the thumbs turn to lift up. Exhale the air you are holding through this open nostril. When this is finished, start the process again for as long as it takes for you to feel better. This type of breathing is popular during yoga meditation.

15. Positive thoughts and their power

The first thing you can do is to become aware that your thoughts are making you anxious. Then, you must interrupt these negative thoughts and place some good ones in your head to stop or interrupt the negative thinking. Some techniques that you might try include the following:

- Think of a person you love and remember the details or qualities that make you love that person.

- Think of something you look forward to doing in the future, like going out to a movie or a great restaurant.
- Carry your favorite book with you, so you can take it out to read when you feel a panic attack beginning.
- Turn on the radio or use your smartphone to play music that can make you happy.
- If you were doing something important during the panic attack, try to go back to it and completely focus on what you were doing.

Use these techniques to interrupt the thinking that makes your panic attack worse. It is important for you to shift your attention away from your anxiety and into something positive that can pull you away from the intensity of your panic attack.

16. Using mindfulness to live in the present

As discussed in the last chapter practicing mindfulness can be very rewarding. Practice being mindful before you have a panic attack so that it becomes second nature to you. To practice mindfulness, you need to do the following things:

- Take yourself to a quiet and pleasant place. Sit down and close your eyes.
- Concentrate on your breathing and how your body feels.
- Shift your focus from your breathing and your body and pay attention to what is around you. Consider what you are hearing, feeling, and smelling. Ask yourself, "What is going on around me?"
- Continue to be mindful and switch back and forth from focusing on your body to what is going on around you until the anxiety begins to fade.

Mindfulness is the best way to bring yourself back to the present. It is also an important tool to use when you are having a panic attack. Mindfulness is about achieving a calm state and extinguishing the rapid-fire negative thinking that goes on during a panic attack. When you are mindful, you are living in the present, and when you live in the present, there is no past or future to worry about.

17. Releasing tension

Doing Progressive Muscle Relaxation (PMR) is a good way to release tension; however, here is another technique you can try while you are having a panic attack (Legg, 2018).

- Find a comfortable place to be, then close your eyes and focus on your breathing. Inhale slowly through your nose, then exhale through your mouth.
- Make a tight fist and squeeze your hand as hard as you can.
- Hold the fist for a few seconds, think of the tension in your hand.
- Open your hand slowly and notice the tension leaving your hand. Feel your hand getting lighter as you relax.
- Try this technique on other parts of your body, like your legs, shoulders, and feet.

18. A simple technique: counting

One of the easiest things to do when you are having a panic attack is to count. When the panic attack starts, make sure that you move yourself to a quiet and safe place to be. If you are doing something like driving or walking in a crowd, take yourself to the side of the road or somewhere safe to sit. Once you are in a safe place, close your eyes and begin counting to ten. It might seem hard to do during your episode, but be patient and keep trying to count to ten. Once you have reached ten, try to get to twenty and so on, until your anxiety goes away.

If you can't close your eyes, you can still count. Continue with the task and count as far as you can, or count the same numbers over and over. Along with counting, don't forget to breathe.

19. Make a plan

Pick a friend or a family member to help you when you have a panic attack and have a plan especially for them to follow. For example, you can have them take you to a quiet and secure place when an episode occurs. You can also teach this person a technique that would help you lower the intensity of your panic attack, such as deep breathing. You can also discuss whether or not this person should consider taking you to the ER. Overall, it is important to have a plan that you can share with a person that you trust.

20. Breathing and your panic attacks

A common symptom of a panic attack is shortness of breath and thoughts of hyperventilating. The way to overcome this is to remember to use your breathing techniques while you are having a panic attack. Learn how to slow your breathing down; in fact, taking a deep breath of air while counting to ten, then counting to ten again when you let out your breath is a good way to combat your shortness of breath. By taking deliberate breaths, you can really help yourself calm down and reduce the intensity of your panic attack (Star, 2020).

21. Cutting down on the intensity of your panic attack

You can call someone on the phone who is prepared to help you when a panic attack episode occurs. You can also try counting to 100 or doing another mental action that can distract you from your panic attack.

22. Manage your time to relieve stress

Break down tasks into manageable pieces and set deadlines to reach them. Don't overcommit to more work than you can handle. It is also good to manage your personal life with a structured schedule that includes downtime or relaxation periods. Don't be afraid to set boundaries with coworkers and people in your personal life, as it is important for you to feel periods of calm as often as possible.

RESOURCES

American Psychiatric Association. (2013). *Diagnostic and Statistical Manual of Mental Disorders* (5th edition). American Psychiatric Association.

Ankrom, S. (2019). Psychotherapy for treating panic disorder. *Verywell Mind.* https://www.verywellmind.com/psychotherapy-for-the-treatment-of-panic-disorder-2584312

Anxiety and Depression Association of America. (n.d.). Facts and Statistics. *Anxiety and Depression Association of America.* https://adaa.org/about-adaa/press-room/facts-statistics

Carbonell, D. (2020). A breathing exercise to calm panic attacks. *Anxiety Coach.* https://www.anxietycoach.com/breathingexercise.html

Carbonell, D. (2020). The key to overcoming panic attacks. *Anxiety Coach.* https://www.anxietycoach.com/overcoming-panic-attacks.html

Carlsen, M. H., Halvorsen, B. L., Holte, K. Bøhn, S. K., Dragland, S., Sampson, L., Willey, C., Senoo, H., Umezono, Y., Sanada, C., Barikmo, I., Berhe, N., Willett, W. C., Phillips, K. M., Jacobs, D. R. Jr., & Blomhoff, R. (2010). The total antioxidant content of more than 3100 foods, beveages, spices, herbs and supplements used worldwide. *Nutrition Journal, 9*, 3. https://doi.org/10.1186/1475-2891-9-3

Cirino, E. (2018). Anxiety exercises to help you relax. *Healthline.* https://www.healthline.com/health/anxiety-exercises

Crawford, J. (2018). How can you stop a panic attack? *Medical News Today.* https://www.medicalnewstoday.com/articles/321510

Elliot, C. H., & Smith, L. L. (2010). *Overcoming anxiety for dummies* (2nd edition). Wiley Publishing Inc.

Exposure therapy. (2015). GoodTherapy. https://www.goodtherapy.org/learn-about-therapy/types/exposure-therapy

Gotter, A. (2018). 11 ways to stop a panic attack. *Healthline.* https://www.healthline.com/health/how-to-stop-a-panic-attack

Gotter, A. (2019). EMDR therapy: What you need to know. *Healthline.* https://www.healthline.com/health/emdr-therapy

Healthline Editorial Team. (2018). Everything you need to know about stress. *Healthline.* https://www.healthline.com/health/stress

Hilmire, M. R., DeVylder, J. E., & Forestell, C. A. (2015). Fermented foods, neuroticism, and social anxiety: An interaction model. *Psychiatry Research, 228*(2), 203-8. https://doi.org/10.1016/j.psychres.2015.04.023

Holmes, L. (2017). Panic attack myths we need to stop believing. *Huffington Post.* https://www.huffingtonpost.ca/entry/panic-attack-myths_n_6509750

How can I prevent panic attacks? (2019). WebMD. https://www.webmd.com/anxiety-panic/how-prevent-panic-attacks#1

How do you feel scared? (n.d.). This Way Up. https://thiswayup.org.au/how-do-you-feel/scared/

How to stop panic attacks? (n.d.). Barends Psychology Practice. https://barendspsychology.com/how-to-stop-panic-attacks/

Katie's story: Recovering from panic attacks, anxiety, and depression. (n.d.). Mental Health Foundation. https://www.mentalhealth.org.uk/stories/katies-story-recovering-panic-attacks-anxiety-and-depression

Mayo Clinic Staff. (n.d.). Panic attacks and panic disorder. *Mayo Clinic.* https://www.mayoclinic.org/diseases-conditions/panic-attacks/symptoms-causes/syc-20376021

Miller, T. (2017). 9 people describe what it feels like to have a panic attack. *Self.* https://www.self.com/story/9-people-describe-what-it-feels-like-to-have-a-panic-attack

Naidoo, U. (2019). Nutritional strategies to ease anxiety. *Harvard Health Publishing.* https://www.health.harvard.edu/blog/nutritional-strategies-to-ease-anxiety-201604139441

Niemiec, R. M. (2017). 3 definitions of mindfulness that might surprise you. *Psychology Today.* https://www.psychologytoday.com/us/blog/what-matters-most/201711/3-definitions-mindfulness-might-surprise-you

Panic and panic attacks. (2019). GoodTherapy. https://www.goodtherapy.org/learn-about-therapy/issues/panic

Rauch, J. (2016). How to handle a panic attack at work: The complete guide. *The Talkspace Voice.* https://www.talkspace.com/blog/how-to-handle-a-panic-attack-at-work-the-complete-guide/

Smith, M., Segal, R., & Segal, J. (2019). Therapy for anxiety disorders. *HelpGuide.* https://www.helpguide.org/articles/anxiety/therapy-for-anxiety-disorders.htm

Star, K. (2019). Cognitive behavioral therapy for panic disorder. *Verywell Mind.* https://www.verywellmind.com/cognitive-behavioral-therapy-2584290

Star, K. (2019). EMDR for panic attacks and anxiety. *Verywell Mind.* https://www.verywellmind.com/emdr-for-panic-disorder-2584292

Star, K. (2016). 7 common myths about panic attacks. *Verywell Mind.* https://www.verywellmind.com/common-myths-about-panic-attacks-2584405

The key to calm: 10 relaxation techniques for panic attacks. (n.d.). Dignity Health. https://www.dignityhealth.org/articles/the-key-to-calm-10-relaxation-techniques-for-panic-attacks

Vandergriendt, C. (2019). What's the difference between a panic attack and an anxiety attack? *Healthline*. https://www.healthline.com/health/panic-attack-vs-anxiety-attack

Ways to stop a panic attack. (2019). WebMD. https://www.webmd.com/anxiety-panic/ss/slideshow-ways-to-stop-panic-attack

YOUR FREE GIFT

Thank you again for purchasing this book. As an additional thank you, you will receive an e-book, as a gift, and completely free.

This guide gives you 14 Days of Mindfulness and sets you on a two-week course to staying present and relaxed. Practice each of the daily prompts to learn more about mindfulness, and add it to your daily routine and meditations.

You can get the bonus booklet as follows:

To access the secret download page, open a browser window on your computer or smartphone and enter: **bonus.derickhowell.com**

You will be automatically directed to the download page.

Please note that this bonus booklet may be only available for download for a limited time.

CPSIA information can be obtained
at www.ICGtesting.com
Printed in the USA
LVHW051018161020
668886LV00008B/274